SKILLS AND VALUES:
LEGAL NEGOTIATING
Second Edition

SKILLS AND VALUES: LEGAL NEGOTIATING

Second Edition

Charles B. Craver
Freda H Alverson Professor
George Washington University Law School

ISBN: 978-0-7698-5278-2 (print)
ISBN: 978-1-5791-1161-8 (eBook)

Library of Congress Cataloging-in-Publication Data

Craver, Charles B
Skills & values. Legal negotiating / Charles B. Craver. — 2nd ed.
p. cm.
    ISBN 978-0-7698-5278-2
        1. Compromise (Law)—United States—Problems, exercises, etc. 2. Negotiation—United States—Problems, exercises, etc. 3. Attorney and client—United States. I. Title. II. Title: Legal negotiating.
KF9084.C73 2012
347.73'9—dc23
 	
<div align="right">2012022493</div>

> NOTE TO USERS
> To ensure that you are using the latest materials available in this area, please be sure to periodically check the LexisNexis Law School web site for downloadable updates and supplements at www.lexisnexis.com/lawschool.

Editorial Offices
121 Chanlon Rd., New Providence, NJ 07974 (908) 464-6800
201 Mission St., San Francisco, CA 94105-1831 (415) 908-3200
www.lexisnexis.com

MATTHEW BENDER

PREFACE

This book can be used alone to teach law students and practicing attorneys legal negotiation skills or as a supplemental resource in conjunction with other texts. It may be used in a Legal Negotiation course, in an Alternative Dispute Resolution or Lawyering Skills class, or as part of a continuing legal education program. Each chapter explores a different aspect of bargaining interactions and provides ways in which readers can explore those issues through practical exercises that are set forth in various chapters.

Many negotiation texts are quite theoretical in scope. They explore economic game theory, psychological phenomena, and other academic theories. They do not directly explain how individuals actually negotiate. This book is designed to fill that void. It covers the different stages of the negotiation process, the various negotiation techniques persons are likely to encounter, the impact of negotiator styles on bargaining interactions, the importance of verbal leaks and nonverbal communication, the way in which gender-based stereotypes may affect bargaining encounters, the unique aspects of telephone and e-mail interactions, international business and human rights negotiations, multi-party interactions, ethical issues negotiators are likely to encounter, and mediation. It thus makes it easy for negotiation students to comprehend how bargaining interactions develop and to appreciate the different factors that affect those encounters.

Students assigned this book can gain access to the LexisNexis Web Course to view videos of lawyers negotiating exercises they may have negotiated and to demonstrate many of the concepts discussed in this book, to see Professor Craver summarizing some of the fundamental areas covered in this text, and to access a Negotiation Preparation Form, a Post Negotiation Evaluation Checklist, and a useful *Summary Guide to Effective Legal Negotiation.*

I have included several negotiation exercises in this book that demonstrate the issues explored in different chapters. Readers should ***not review the exercises until they are prepared to work with someone else on them.*** If they look at the **Confidential Information** for both sides, it would make it difficult for them to work on the exercises in an unbiased manner. When readers are prepared to work on a particular exercise, they and their partners should agree upon the sides they will represent. They should both read the **General Information**, but only read their own side's **Confidential Information**. This will enable them to proceed as if they are really representing their assigned party. Following each multiple item exercise is an efficiency grid that demonstrates the way in which bargainers should have resolved the so-called cooperative or integrative terms if they wished to achieve efficient agreements that maximized the joint returns obtained by the negotiating parties. A number of additional negotiation exercises are also included in the Teacher's Manual which allows instructors to assign exercises for which readers cannot see the Confidential Information pages until they are actually disclosed.

Charles B. Craver
Washington, D.C.

TABLE OF CONTENTS

TABLE OF CONTENTS

TABLE OF CONTENTS

TABLE OF CONTENTS

Chapter 1
INTRODUCTION

I. IMPORTANCE OF NEGOTIATION SKILLS

Lawyers negotiate constantly. They negotiate even when they do not appreciate the fact they are involved with bargaining encounters. Students negotiate to obtain interviews with firms and government agencies. The interviews involve negotiation skills, as the interviewees endeavor to convince the firm or agency attorneys that they should hire these candidates. Once employment offers are obtained, candidates should politely ask whether the parties may negotiate over the terms being offered. In some cases, salary gains may be achieved. Even where firms have set salary policies, those entities may be willing to pay for bar review courses, the costs of taking the bar examinations, moving expenses, and the cost of attending continuing legal education programs that will enhance the lawyering skills of these new associates.

New associates negotiate with their partners, associates, legal assistants, and others within their own firms and agencies. Associates negotiate when they interact with prospective clients and with current clients. They also negotiate when they interact with others on behalf of their own clients.

The vast majority of legal disputes are disposed of through negotiated settlement agreements. In most states, fewer than five percent of civil and criminal matters are adjudicated. The remaining ninety-five percent are dismissed, withdrawn, or resolved through negotiated arrangements. Even with respect to the few cases that are actually litigated, the lawyers can employ their negotiation skills to narrow the legal and factual issues and to streamline the discovery process.

Business transactions are almost always structured through bargaining discussions. Buy/sell arrangements, commercial property transactions, patent/copyright licensing terms, joint ventures, international business deals, and similar arrangements are all structured through negotiations.

II. LIMITED LAW SCHOOL TREATMENT

Law schools do an excellent job of teaching students how to think like lawyers. Through the use of different hypothetical fact patterns and Socratic questioning, law teachers demonstrate how slight changes in factual matters can significantly influence legal conclusions. Students learn how to ask the questions that will lead them to the cogent analysis of legal dilemmas.

Law schools have traditionally had few formal courses designed to teach students how to prepare for and conduct legal negotiations. As recently as ten or fifteen years ago, many schools did not even offer courses on Legal Negotiating. Faculty members thought that such skills courses did not fit within their theoretical and sophisticated curricula. Law professors seemed to believe that students either knew how to negotiate from their prior endeavors, or would learn such practical skills once they entered practice.

Almost all law schools have begun to appreciate how important negotiation skills are and the need to teach such skills to law students. Some now have first year lawyering skills courses that include client counseling, legal research and writing, and negotiation. Others incorporate negotiation skills training in Alternative Dispute Resolution courses, while others have separate courses devoted to negotiation practice.

Negotiation courses must be both practical and theoretical, and they are highly interdisciplinary. Individuals can read everything ever written on the negotiation process and not improve their bargaining skills. They can alternatively engage in numerous negotiation exercises without gaining a real appreciation of the factors that influence bargaining encounters. Negotiation involves an *experiential lawyering skill* that must be learned both through an understanding of the theoretical underpinnings and through exercises designed to teach students the practical application of the underlying concepts being explored.

Negotiation students have to appreciate the impact of psychological and sociological concepts, the importance of verbal and nonverbal communication, and the application of economic game theory. They have to appreciate the structured nature of bargaining interactions, to enable them to know what they should be trying to accomplish during each separate stage of the process. They need to understand the different negotiating techniques, both to enable them to decide which tactics they should employ in particular circumstances and to recognize and effectively counteract the techniques being employed against them.

What personal characteristics make individuals proficient negotiators? Are better students more effective negotiators? Although one might think that better students should achieve better negotiation results than less proficient students based upon their supposed intellectual superiority, I have found no correlation between student GPAs and the results they achieve on negotiation exercises.[1] It is important to recognize that GPAs reflect student abstract reasoning skills, while negotiation results reflect student interpersonal skills. I have had students in my Legal Negotiation course at the top of their graduating classes, and you would not want to have them negotiate a parking ticket for you. On the other hand, I have had students in my class who graduated near the bottom of their classes, and you would not want to negotiate against them.

Several years ago, I worked with psychologist Allison Abbe to determine whether students with higher emotional intelligence scores achieved more beneficial results on negotiation exercises. In our unpublished study, we found no meaningful correlation between emotional intelligence scores and student performance. Although Daniel Goleman has suggested that if IQ scores do not account for certain results, emotional intelligence (EQ) scores most likely do so,[2] we were unable to discern any meaningful correlation between either IQ or EQ scores with respect to student negotiating performance.

---

[1] *See* Charles B. Craver, *The Impact of Student GPAs and a Pass/Fail Option on Clinical Negotiation Course Performance*, 15 Oʜɪᴏ Sᴛ. J. Dɪsᴘ. Rᴇs. 373 (2000). The pass/fail students did substantially less well on the negotiation exercises than the graded students, due to the fact the grades attained by the graded students were directly affected by their results on negotiation exercises compared to the results achieved by their classmates. When exercise participants had to decide whether to spend extra time preparing for interactions or negotiating with others, the graded students were willing to spend the additional time, but the pass/fail students were not. *See also* Charles B. Craver, *Clinical Negotiating Achievement as a Function of Traditional Law School Success and as a Predictor of Future Negotiating Performance*, 1986 Mᴏ. J. Dɪsᴘ. Rᴇs. 63 (1986).

[2] *See generally* Dᴀɴɪᴇʟ Gᴏʟᴇᴍᴀɴ, Sᴏᴄɪᴀʟ Iɴᴛᴇʟʟɪɢᴇɴᴄᴇ (2006); Dᴀɴɪᴇʟ Gᴏʟᴇᴍᴀɴ, Eᴍᴏᴛɪᴏɴᴀʟ Iɴᴛᴇʟʟɪɢᴇɴᴄᴇ (1995).

Skilled negotiators usually outperform less skilled bargainers. They know how to prepare for such interactions, and they know what to do during each stage of the process. They know what tactics to employ and how to counter the techniques being used against them. This enables them to exude an ***inner confidence*** that disconcerts less certain opponents. When I ask less successful students in my negotiation class why they gave in to opponent demands, they often indicate that their adversaries were not really great negotiators — those persons simply seemed so certain they were right these individuals thought they were wrong. What the less successful negotiators did not appreciate was the fact that the confidence of their opponents caused them to doubt their own initial assessments and induced them to move in the direction of the other side.

Proficient negotiators know how to place themselves in the shoes of their opponents to enable them to estimate the factors influencing those parties and to think about how low or high those persons should be willing to go. Adept bargainers also ask far more questions during bargaining interactions than their less successful cohorts. This enables them to obtain more important information from their adversaries than they disclose.

Most Americans are not naturally skilled negotiators. We are not a negotiating culture. Few of us regularly go to commercial markets and negotiate the terms of our transactions. We go to supermarkets and other retail stores and pay the stated prices or refrain from buying the items in question. In many other cultures, however, all of these prices are negotiable. Citizens in these countries negotiate constantly with respect to almost everything they need. As a result, they are comfortable with the bargaining process, and they actually look forward to negotiation situations.

Americans should not fear bargaining encounters, nor should they view them as unpleasant experiences. They should instead view such encounters as ***opportunities*** providing them with the chance to improve their current situations. If the other side did not have the ability to enhance their circumstances, the parties would not be negotiating.

Several years ago, the mother of one of my Legal Negotiation students came to Washington, D.C. to visit. They went to that Middle-Eastern Negotiation Bazar known as Nordstrom's Department Store. The mother found an outfit she liked and asked the salesperson if that was the best price she could provide. The daughter was mortified, suggesting that such behavior was completely inappropriate in a store like Nordstrom's. The clerk then indicated that the outfit would go on sale the following Monday with a twenty-five percent price reduction. She told the mother to return on Monday to obtain the sales price. The mother replied that she was visiting her daughter and would be returning home the coming weekend. The clerk then said that if the mother allowed her to ring up the outfit at the full price now, she could provide her with a twenty-five percent rebate on her credit card when the sales price went into the computer on Monday. The parties had a deal, the mother saved twenty-five percent, and the daughter was no longer mortified!

It is amazing how often if persons politely ask if something is negotiable they will be offered more beneficial terms. Law students should appreciate this fact and view negotiation encounters as opportunities to enhance their situations or the situations of their clients. They have been negotiating for many years with their parents, siblings, friends, and even strangers, but they have not thought about these regular occurrences. They have forgotten the many tools they learned intuitively as children. Legal Negotiation courses simply provide them with the opportunity to rethink ideas they learned as children and to learn new concepts that will enhance the skills they already possess.

III. ETHICAL CONSIDERATIONS

As course participants work on the negotiation exercises in this book, they should consider the ethical implications of their actions.[3] It is common at the beginning of interactions for negotiators to demand more or offer less than they really hope to obtain or are willing to pay. Individuals requesting money embellish their circumstances, while those being asked to provide money understate the value of the transactions being discussed. Does such behavior contravene the ethical standards applicable to attorneys? Although we will explore this topic in depth in Chapter 20, it is important to recognize here that Model Rule 4.1 provides that "a lawyer shall not knowingly: (a) make a false statement or material fact or law to a third person."

Rule 4.1(a) would appear to proscribe exaggeration, puffing, and embellishment. Nonetheless, Comment 2 acknowledges the different expectations indigenous to bargaining encounters. "Under generally accepted conventions in negotiation, certain types of statements ordinarily are not taken as statements of material fact. Estimates of price or value placed on the subject of a transaction and a party's intentions as to an acceptable settlement of a claim are ordinarily in this category . . ." It is thus ethical for negotiators to demand more or offer less than they are willing to accept or pay. It is similarly ethical for negotiators to under- or over-state the value of items being discussed for strategic purposes. When the opposing side asks for Item 1, this side may indicate a reluctance to give up that item even when that issue has no value to them. They do this hoping to obtain a concession from the other side in exchange for Item 1 which the other side does value.

It is ironic that Comment 2 permits negotiators to misrepresent their side's *settlement intentions* and how they *value the items being exchanged*, since these are the most material matters during bargaining interactions. The facts, law, economic, political, and cultural issues are all secondary. What each negotiator must truly ascertain concerns two fundamental issues: (1) what does the other side really want; and (2) how much of each item must this side give up to induce the opposing side to enter into a mutual accord.

As readers work on the various negotiation exercises, they should contemplate the difference between acceptable puffing and embellishment and unacceptable misrepresentation of material fact. Individuals who make false statements that are not exempt from Rule 4.1 coverage will develop negative reputations among class members, and this fact will usually affect them negatively when they subsequently interact with the same opponents *or* with other persons who have been informed of their questionable behavior.

---

[3] *See generally* Charles B. Craver, *Negotiation Ethics for Real World Interactions*, 25 Ohio St. J. Disp. Res. 299 (2010).

Chapter 2
SILENT NEGOTIATION EXERCISE

Students often indicate that they have never negotiated before, ignoring prior interactions with parents, siblings, friends, and many others. Everything they need to know to be a good negotiator they learned before Kindergarten.[1] Children are quite persistent, and they often play one parent off against the other. Children intuitively recognize that there is no such thing as bargaining power, but only the perception of it. If they can ignore the objectively superior bargaining power possessed by their parents, children can effectively counteract it. Children are also taught that you get more with honey than with vinegar, causing them to appreciate the fact that they should not behave badly when they negotiate if they hope to achieve their bargaining objectives.

When students and attorneys are asked to work on negotiation exercises, they begin with esoteric discussions of the operative facts and relevant legal issues. As their interactions progress, however, neither side accepts the other's factual and legal assertions. At a certain point, the negotiators begin to ignore these matters and focus on how much money one hopes to obtain and the other is willing to pay. They assert that the actual exercise details become completely irrelevant to their discussions. When this happens, I often divide the class into pairs and give each pair $100,000. I give them five minutes to agree upon an appropriate division of the money. The students then ask which side they are on and which party should pay money to the other. I remind them of their claim that the particular details of exercises do not influence their interactions and tell them to do what they think is appropriate. At this point, the students realize that the specific facts provided in each exercise and the operative legal issues really do affect their negotiations. While it may appear that neither side openly accepts the other side's factual and legal assertions, their willingness to pay or accept certain amounts of money is directly related to the exercise they are engaged in.

I always assign the following *silent exercise* to demonstrate how difficult it is for parties to negotiate when the only item they may communicate about is money. I not only disclose the General Information describing the operative facts, but also explain each side's Confidential Information in front of both sides. I want to be sure that both sides are fully aware of the factors influencing their opponents and appreciate how low the Plaintiff is willing to go and how high the Defendant is willing to go.

SILENT NEGOTIATION EXERCISE

An unmarried twenty-year old female Plaintiff was injured in an automobile accident with the Defendant. Due to flying glass, the Plaintiff lost the sight in one eye and suffered permanent facial scars. She still suffers from occasional bad headaches. Her unpaid medical bills to date amount to $20,000. The Defendant has admitted negligence, but has alleged contributory negli-

---

[1] *See* Charles B. Craver, *Everything You Need to Know to Be a Great Negotiator You Learned Before Kindergarten,* THE NEGOTIATOR MAGAZINE, April 2005, *available at* http://www.negotiatormagazine.com/article248_1_html.

gence by the Plaintiff. When this case arose many years ago in the State of Michigan, it was still a contributory negligence jurisdiction. A law suit for $300,000 has been filed.

NEGOTIATION INSTRUCTIONS

Readers should be divided into pairs with one half deemed Plaintiffs and the other half Defendants. They have three minutes to reach an agreement. They may **not talk** at all. The only way they may communicate is in writing and they may only **write down monetary figures** — demands by the Plaintiffs and offers by the Defendants. No other communication of any kind may be employed.

CONFIDENTIAL INFORMATION FOR PLAINTIFF

CONFIDENTIAL INFORMATION FOR PLAINTIFF

Your client is financially destitute and emotionally distraught. The accident, the injuries, the medical bills, and the pending litigation have drained her financially and psychologically. She has recently been seeing a psychiatrist and is prepared to put this entire incident behind her. The headaches have abated, but her mental state has deteriorated due to the pending litigation. She wants to obtain $20,000 to pay off her medical bills and be through with everything. Her psychiatrist has informed you, with her permission, that if this case is not resolved quickly, she is likely to suffer an emotional relapse and commit suicide. The Plaintiff has instructed you to settle this matter immediately for any amount over $20,000. You should assume that you are representing the Plaintiff on a pro bono, no-fee basis, thus she will obtain any sum agreed upon to settle this case.

SELF-ASSESSMENT

SELF-ASSESSMENT

When the time limit has expired, I tell the participants to cease negotiating and ask them how many have not reached any agreement. About 20–25 percent usually raise their hands. I ask these persons how many rejected offers between $20,000 and $300,000, and almost all raise their hands. I then talk about how overtly competitive many negotiation interactions are and the fact participants do not wish to be embarrassed in front of their peers. The silent negotiators thus put down different numbers hoping their opponents move in their direction. If this does not occur, they usually put down one last number with about ten seconds remaining, hoping the other side will be risk-averse and give in. Unfortunately, their opponents did not. As a result, the Plaintiff representatives have a dead client and the Defendant representatives have been terminated — but at least neither side was embarrassed!

I ask if any pairs settled for exactly $160,000, which is half way between $20,000 and $300,000. I occasionally get one group to raise their hands, and I ask if the negotiators reached this mid-point deliberately. Some say that they did so, because they knew this would be "fair." I ask the plaintiffs if they would be willing to accept the loss of one eye and permanent facial scars in exchange for $160,000. They pull back and respond negatively. I then ask whether they still consider the $160,000 figure to be "fair." Most are quite honest and begin to realize that the mid-point between their positions does not necessarily produce a "fair" result. I quickly point out that this figure is "fair" given the parameters of the negotiation exercise, but note that the mid-point between the parties bottom lines does not necessarily generate truly "fair" agreements from the perspective of the adversely affected claimants.

I then ask how many pairs settled for less than $50,000, from $50,000-$100,000, from $100,000 to $150,000, from, $150,000 to $200,000, from, $200,000 to $250,000, and for over $250,000. I usually have settlements in all six categories.

I then talk about how differently individuals evaluate identical information, demonstrated by the settlements that range from about $25,000 to $275,000 when both sides were fully aware of other side's Confidential Information.

I next talk about how difficult it is to negotiate when parties can only exchange monetary offers, and emphasize the importance of factual, legal, and economic discussions to lubricate settlement discussions and keep the process moving between concessions. It takes time for parties to realize that they should change their positions, and the negotiators have to talk about different issues while they are debating internally whether to announce new offers and demands.

I finally note that less proficient negotiators tend to focus almost entirely on their **own side's needs,** while more skilled negotiators look across the bargaining table and try to estimate the **other side's needs and interests** to help them determine how well they can do. If a Plaintiff representative hopes to obtain a large amount of money, she wants the Defendant to focus on one thing: any amount under $300,000 is acceptable to that side. If the Defendant representative wants to pay a small sum, he wants the Plaintiff to focus on one thing: any amount over $20,000 is acceptable. I then point out how they must not only focus on their own side's needs, but also estimate the needs and interests of their opponents. How high or low do they think the other side is willing to go? What are the other side's strengths and weaknesses? It is only through this exploration process that they can truly begin to appreciate the actual bargaining power they possess and determine how much or how little they may have to agree upon if they wish to achieve mutual accords.

Chapter 3
NEGOTIATION PROCESS

When people prepare for bargaining encounters, they spend hours on the factual issues, the legal issues, the economic issues, and the political issues. How much time do they spend on their actual negotiation strategy? Usually no more than ten to fifteen minutes. When they begin an interaction, most negotiators have only three things in mind relating to their bargaining strategy: (1) where they plan to begin; (2) where they hope to end up; and (3) their bottom line. Between their opening offer and the conclusion of their encounter, most individuals "wing it," thinking of the interaction as wholly unstructured. If they only understood how structured bargaining transactions are, they would know what to do during each stage of the process.

In this section, we will explore the six distinct stages of the negotiation process: (1) preparation; (2) establishment of negotiator identities and the tone for the interaction; (3) information exchange; (4) exchange of items to be divided; (5) closing the deal; and (6) maximizing the joint returns. We will discuss the purpose of each stage and the most effective ways to accomplish the objectives underling each.

I. PREPARATION (ESTABLISHING LIMITS AND GOALS)

If you know the enemy and know yourself, you need not fear the result of a hundred battles. If you know yourself but not the enemy, for every victory gained you will also suffer a defeat. If you know neither the enemy nor yourself, you will succumb in every battle.[1]

Persons who thoroughly prepare for bargaining encounters generally achieve more beneficial results than those who do not, because knowledge constitutes power at the bargaining table.[2] Well prepared negotiators possess the knowledge they need to value their impending interactions, and they exude a greater confidence in their positions than their adversaries. Their confidence undermines the conviction of less prepared opponents and causes those persons to question their own positions. As less prepared advocates subconsciously defer to the greater certainty exhibited by their more knowledgeable adversaries, these less prepared participants tend to make more frequent and greater concessions.

A. Client Preparation

When attorneys are asked to negotiate on behalf of clients, those legal representatives must elicit all of the relevant factual information possessed by their clients.[3]

They must also determine what those clients hope to achieve through legal representation. Clients frequently fail to disclose their real underlying interests and objectives when they talk with lawyers, because they only consider options they think attorneys can obtain for them. It is thus critical for lawyers to carefully probe client interests and goals, and to listen intently to client responses.[4]

---

[1] SUN TZU, THE ART OF WAR 43 (J. Clavell ed., Delta 1983).

[2] See GAVIN KENNEDY, ESSENTIAL NEGOTIATION 176–77 (2d ed. 2009); BARGAINING: FORMAL THEORIES OF NEGOTIATION 10-11 (Oran R. Young ed., 1975).

[3] See JOHN LANDE, LAWYERING WITH PLANNED EARLY NEGOTIATION 86–89 (2011).

[4] See Leonard L. Riskin, *The Contemplative Lawyer: On the Potential Contributions of Mindfulness*

Persons who say they wish to purchase or lease specific commercial property may suggest that they are only interested in that location. When these people are asked probing questions regarding their intended use, it may become apparent that alternative locations may be acceptable. Knowledge about these alternatives enhances this side's bargaining power by providing viable options if the current discussions do not progress satisfactorily. Clients contemplating the investment of resources in other firms should be asked about their ultimate objectives. Are they willing to invest their assets in a single venture, or would they prefer to diversify their holdings? Are they willing to risk their capital to achieve a higher return or would they prefer a less generous return on an investment that is likely to preserve their initial investment? Is a business seller willing to accept future cash payments, shares of stock in the purchasing firm, or in-kind payments in goods or services provided by the purchasing company?

Clients who initially ask for monetary relief through the litigation process may have failed to consider alternative interests. Someone contemplating a defamation action may prefer a retraction and a public apology to protracted litigation. A person who thinks she was wrongfully discharged from employment may prefer reinstatement and a transfer to another department instead of a substantial monetary sum. A victim of alleged sexual harassment may prefer an apology and stay-away promise from the harasser to monetary compensation and likely future difficulties. If attorneys do not ascertain the real underlying interests of their clients, they may ignore options that may enhance their bargaining positions and help them achieve optimal agreements.[5]

As lawyers explore client interests and objectives, they must try to determine the degree to which the clients want the different items to be exchanged. Most legal representatives formally or informally divide client goals into three categories: (1) essential; (2) important; and (3) desirable. *Essential* items include terms clients must obtain if agreements are to be successfully achieved. *Important* goals concern things clients really want to acquire, but which they would be willing to exchange for essential or other important items. *Desirable* needs involve items of secondary value which clients would be pleased to obtain, but which they would exchange for "essential" or "important" terms.

For each item to be negotiated, attorneys should try to determine how much clients value different levels of attainment.[6] For example, money may be an "essential" issue for a person who has sustained serious injuries in an automobile accident. The client may consider the first $200,000 critical, both to make up for lost earnings and to enable her to pay off unpaid medical bills and increased credit card debt. While the client would like to obtain more than $200,000, she may only consider amounts above $200,000 "important," rather than "essential." As a result, the client may not consider $400,000 to be twice as beneficial as the initial $200,000. Her lawyer may have to obtain $500,000 or even $600,000 before the client would consider the sum achieved twice as good as the first $200,000. Lawyers preparing for bargaining encounters must make these calculations for *each item* to be negotiated. Only by

---

Meditation to Law Students, Lawyers, and Their Clients, 7 HARV. NEGOT. L. REV. 601, 649–650 (2002); ABRAHAM P. ORDOVER & ANDREA DONEFF, ALTERNATIVES TO LITIGATION 32–33 (2002).

[5] *See* ROGER FISHER & WILLIAM URY, GETTING TO YES 101–11 (1981).

[6] *See* HOWARD RAIFFA, NEGOTIATION ANALYSIS: THE SCIENCE AND ART OF COLLABORATIVE DECISION MAKING 129–147 (2003).

appreciating the degree to which the client values different amounts of particular commodities can they hope to obtain results that will most effectively satisfy the client's underlying interests.

Attorneys must similarly ascertain the relative values of the various items to be negotiated within each broad category. Does the client value Item A twice as much as Item B or two-thirds as much? How does Item C compare to Items A and B? It helps to mentally assign point values to the various items to enable legal representatives to understand how they can maximize overall client satisfaction. Legal advocates can use this relative value information to decide which items to seek and which items to trade for other terms the client values more highly. In most of the negotiation exercises set forth in this book, point values have been assigned to the different items to be exchanged. Negotiators should recognize that these assigned points represent their client value systems. Negotiators should strive to maximize the degree of satisfaction they obtain for their assigned clients. These assigned point values also make it easy for negotiators to determine how well they did vis-a-vis other negotiators and how efficiently they and their opponents divided the items involved.

When determining client objectives, lawyers should avoid the substitution of their own values for those of their clients, realizing that client interests must guide their negotiation strategy. Negotiating lawyers should not be constrained by judicial authority or usual business practices. Negotiators can agree to any terms that are legal. Clients often prefer results that could not be achieved through adjudications (*e.g.*, retractions in defamation actions or apologies in harassment cases) or which might not be consistent with usual business arrangements (*e.g.*, in-kind payments). Lawyers should not ignore these possibilities merely because courts could not award them or many business leaders would not approve them.

B.   Lawyer Preparation

Once lawyers have ascertained the relevant factual information and the underlying interests and goals of their clients, they must become thoroughly familiar with the relevant legal doctrines, economic aspects, and, where pertinent, political agendas. They must develop cogent legal theories to support their positions, and anticipate the counter-arguments they expect opposing counsel to make. Negotiators confronted by anticipated claims are unlikely to have their confidence undermined by those contentions.

1.   *Calculating Own and Opposing Side's Bottom Lines*

After attorneys become familiar with the relevant factual and legal matters affecting their own side, they must determine their bottom line — *i.e.*, their Best Alternative to a Negotiated Agreement (BATNA).[7] What are the best results they could realistically hope to obtain through other channels? It is critical for negotiators to have a set bottom line to be certain they will not enter into agreements that would be worse than what would happen if no accords were obtained.[8]

---

[7] *See* Fisher & Ury, *supra* note 5, at 101–111. Some litigators, especially defendants, use the term WATNA (Worst Alternative to a Negotiated Agreement) to establish their bottom line. Economic game theorists often use the terms "reservation point" or "resistence point."

[8] *See* Russell Korobkin, *A Positive Theory of Legal Negotiation*, 88 Geo. L.J. 1789, 1797 (2000); Samfrits Le Poole, Never Take No for an Answer 60–61 (2d ed. 1991).

Negotiators who are initially unable to evaluate the results of nonsettlements must take the time to develop alternatives. This is especially important for transactional experts. Their client may be seeking a buy-sell agreement with a single firm or a licensing arrangement with one party. Are there other potential purchasers or sellers they should contact? Other potential license partners? As alternatives become numerous, lawyers and their clients may wish to create decision trees that graphically depict the strengths and weaknesses associated with each option.[9] Each limb represents a different alternative, with the advantages and disadvantages of each option being listed with the likelihood of obtaining those results. This visual approach makes it easier for many individuals to appreciate the comparative values of the different options.

Table 3-1 provides a decision tree pertaining to a medical malpractice case.

TABLE 3-1 PLAINTIFF DECISION TREE
MEDICAL MALPRACTICE CASE

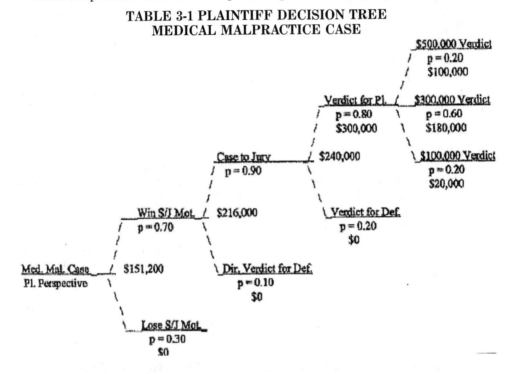

The projected value for this case from the Plaintiff's perspective would be $151,200 — the sum of the various branches of the decision tree. Due to an "egocentric bias," claimant attorneys tend to over-estimate likely jury outcomes, while defense lawyers tend to under-estimate such outcomes.[10] (Two critical factors bring the two sides closer together. First, the fact that plaintiffs usually focus on their downside risks (losing or obtaining lower verdicts), while defendants focus on their upside risks (losing large awards). The second factor concerns the impact of transaction costs.

The monetary and non-monetary transactional costs associated with settlement and nonsettlement must also be considered. Litigants must recognize that the monetary

---

[9] *See generally* JOHN S. HAMMOND, RALPH L. KEENEY & HOWARD RAIFFA, SMART CHOICES: A PRACTICAL GUIDE TO MAKING BETTER DECISIONS (1999).

[10] *See* RAIFFA, *supra* note 6, at 146–47.

and psychological costs of trial must be *subtracted from* the anticipated plaintiff's outcome, because these costs would diminish the value of any plaintiff judgment.[11] Since the defendant would have to incur these costs no matter who prevails at trial, these defense costs have to be *added to* the defendant's expected result.

A similar expected-value analysis should be performed by persons preparing for transactional encounters. Suppose the owner of a firm is deciding how much they should expect to obtain from the sale of their corporation. Let's assume the owner believes there is a 10 percent chance the business will sell for $50 million, a 30 percent chance it will sell for at least $45 million, a 60 percent chance it will sell for at least $40 million, a 90 percent chance it will sell for at least $35 million, and a 100 percent chance it will sell for at least $30 million. What would be the expected value of the firm?

0.10 (10%) × $50,000,000	$5,000,000
0.20 (30% - 10%) × $45,000,000	$9,000,000
0.30 (60% - 30%) × $40,000,000	$12,000,000
0.30 (90% - 60%) × $35,000,000	$10,500,000
0.10 (100% - 90%) × $30,000,000	$3,000,000
Expected Value:	$39,500,000

The client must now be asked how much money she really has to obtain to sell her business. She may have to have at least $35 million, and would not accept anything below that figure. How willing is she to hold out for the possibility of a higher amount? The attorney and client must determine how risk averse or risk taking the client is willing to be. A risk taker may be willing to hold out for $45 million, while a risk averse seller may not be able to hold out much past $40 million.

Once attorneys have determined their own side's expected value, they often think they have completed this part of the evaluative process. The many lawyers who come to this conclusion ignore an equally important part of the preliminary equation: their ***opponent's expected value***.[12] Legal representatives should employ formal and informal discovery techniques to obtain the relevant information possessed by the opposing party. They must ascertain, to the degree they can before they begin to directly interact with those individuals, the needs and interests of their adversaries. This will allow them to predict the items they want that are of minimal importance to the other side, and which terms the other side wants that are not valued by their own client. They must also attempt to determine the alternatives available to the other side if no agreement is achieved through the current negotiations. If the other side's nonsettlement options are worse than this party's external options, this side has greater bargaining power. The cost of a nonsettlement to this side is less onerous than the cost of nonconcurrence to the other party. An appreciation of opponent nonsettlement alternatives also allows this side to prepare a negotiation strategy that will culminate in an offer that should be preferable to the opposing side's nonsettlement options.

---

[11] Even if the plaintiff is suing under a fee-shifting statute that authorizes awards of attorney fees to prevailing plaintiffs (e.g., Title VII of the Civil Rights Act of 1964, 42 U.S.C. § 2000e-5(k) (2000)), they may have other monetary costs and will have definite nonmonetary costs that still have to be considered.

[12] *See* GRANDE LUM, THE NEGOTIATION FIELDBOOK 58 (2d ed. 2011); Korobkin, *supra* note 8, at 1797–99.

2. *Establishing Elevated Aspiration Levels*

Attorneys preparing for bargaining encounters must recognize that persons who begin their interactions with elevated goals obtain more beneficial results than individuals who begin with modest objectives.[13] These goals should always be well above their bottom lines if negotiators hope to obtain optimal results.[14] Bargainers should not establish modest objectives merely to avoid the possibility they might not obtain everything they want.[15] While high aspiration bargainers might not achieve their ultimate goals, they usually obtain better results than negotiators with lower objectives. Persons who always get what they want when they negotiate should realize that their successes may reflect their unduly modest objectives. They should thus raise their goals for future encounters by five to ten percent. If these persons continue to obtain everything they want, they should continue to raise their goals. They should continue this incremental process until they begin to obtain less than they hoped to get. At this point, these individuals have probably learned to establish appropriately elevated objectives.

Consistently successful negotiators establish elevated aspiration levels before they commence interactions with opponents. They ascertain the pertinent factual, legal, and economic issues, and estimate the most generous results they could reasonably hope to obtain. They then increase their objectives and work diligently to formulate arguments that make their seemingly excessive goals seem reasonable. Less certain adversaries tend to defer to the overt confidence exuded by these more thoroughly prepared participants.[16]

Proficient negotiators focus primarily on their *aspiration levels* when they bargain. They only rely upon their *bottom lines* when they have to decide whether to continue interactions that appear to be unproductive. Less skilled bargainers tend to focus excessively on their bottom lines throughout their interactions. Once they attain these minimal objectives, they relax knowing that some agreement will be achieved, and they no longer work hard to surpass their bottom-lines. Observant opponents can discern their relaxed states and become less generous with respect to subsequent concessions. These bottom-line oriented negotiators thus settle for less generous terms than their cohorts who continue to focus on their aspiration levels throughout their bargaining interactions.[17]

When individuals prepare for negotiation encounters, they should establish generous — but *realistically attainable* — objectives. If their goals are entirely unreasonable, they may discourage opponents and induce those persons to think that mutually acceptable agreements are unattainable.[18] Unusually elevated aspiration bargainers may encounter an additional problem. Once they get into the negotiation and realize that their objectives are not achievable, they may lose this important touchstone and move quickly toward their bottom lines.

---

[13] *See* Russell Korobkin, *Aspirations and Settlement*, 88 CORNELL L. REV. 1, 4, 20-30 (2002); ROGER DAWSON, SECRETS OF POWER NEGOTIATING 16–17 (3d ed. 2011); MAX H. BAZERMAN & MARGARET A. NEALE, NEGOTIATING RATIONALLY 28 (Free Press 1992).

[14] *See* LEPOOLE, *supra* note 8, at 62–63.

[15] *See* RICHARD SHELL, BARGAINING FOR ADVANTAGE 32–33 (Viking 1999).

[16] *See* Jennifer Gerarda Brown, *The Role of Hope in Negotiation*, 44 U.C.L.A. L. REV. 1661, 1675 (1997).

[17] *See* SHELL, *supra* note 15, at 24–32.

[18] *See* Korobkin, *supra* note 13, at 62-63.

3. *Formulating Elevated but Principled Opening Offers*

Advocates who commence bargaining interactions with raised expectations recognize that it is impossible for even skilled negotiators to accurately calculate the value of impending encounters solely from their own side's perspective. Until they begin to interact with their opponents, they are not certain regarding the degree to which those individuals want or need the prospective deal.

Many persons are hesitant to formulate excessive opening positions for fear of offending their opponents. Nonetheless, proficient negotiators attempt to develop the most beneficial positions they can rationally defend.[19] They realize that if their initial offers are wholly unrealistic, they will feel awkward when they try to justify their positions and undermine their credibility. On the other hand, they understand that if they begin with modest offers, they immediately place themselves at a disadvantage.

Some individuals commence bargaining encounters with modest proposals hoping to generate reciprocal behavior by their opponents. Opening offers that are overly generous to adversaries are likely to have the opposite effect due to the impact of a phenomenon known as *"anchoring."*[20] When people receive better offers than they anticipated, they question their own preliminary assessments and *increase* their own aspiration levels. They expect to obtain more beneficial results than they initially thought possible, and they make initial offers more favorable to their own side.

When negotiators formulate their initial offers, they should develop principled rationales they can use to explain how they arrived at their stated positions.[21] Litigators should thus carefully explain the exact basis for their offers. How have they valued the past and expected future medical expenses and compensation loses? How have they valued the pain and suffering? Transactional bargainers should do the same thing. How have they valued the real property, building and equipment, accounts receivable, patents and trade marks, good will, etc.? The development of specific values for each of the components to be discussed supported by logical explanations demonstrates a firm commitment to the overall positions being articulated.[22] It also makes it more difficult for opponents to dismiss such positions without careful consideration of the supporting rationales.[23] A principled opening offer often allows the initiating party to accomplish one other important objective — it may enable that party to define the bargaining agenda.

4. *Choreographing the Impending Interaction*

Once legal representatives have determined their bottom lines, aspiration levels, and opening offers, they must plan their bargaining strategies. How do they envision moving from where they begin to where they would like to conclude their encounter? Do they anticipate a number of small concessions or a few large position changes?

---

[19] *See* SHELL, *supra* note 15, at 160–61.

[20] *See* Korobkin, *supra* note 13, at 30-36; SHELL, *supra* note 15, at 161–62; Russell Korobkin & Chris Guthrie, *Psychological Barriers to Litigation Settlement: An Experimental Approach*, 93 MICH. L. REV. 107, 138–42 (1994).

[21] *See* JAMES C. FREUND, SMART NEGOTIATING 122–23 (1992); JOHN ILICH, DEAL-BREAKERS & BREAK-THROUGHS 112 (1992).

[22] *See* STEFAN H. KRIEGER, RICHARD K. NEUMANN, JR., KATHLEEN H. MCMANUS & STEVEN D. JAMAR, ESSENTIAL LAWYERING SKILLS 282–83 (1999).

[23] *See* ANTHONY R. PRATKANIS & ELLIOT ARONSON, AGE OF PROPAGANDA 26–27 (1991).

What bargaining techniques do they think would most effectively move their opponents toward their objectives? At what point during their interaction do they plan to take a firm stand, hoping to generate beneficial final terms? The more negotiators visualize a successful transition from their opening positions to their desired results, the more likely they are to be successful.

Proficient negotiators appreciate the importance of planning to reach ultimate offers that will be considered attractive by reasonably risk averse opponents. If their offers are wholly unacceptable, it is easy for adversaries to accept the less onerous consequences associated with nonsettlements. On the other hand, most people find it difficult to reject definitive offers that are at least as good as what they think they might achieve through their nonsettlement alternatives.

When individuals prepare for bargaining encounters, the following Negotiation Preparation Form may be helpful.

NEGOTIATION PREPARATION FORM

1. Your *minimum settlement point [BATNA]* — Lowest result you would accept given your alternatives to negotiated settlement (including *transaction costs* associated with both settlement and non-settlement):

2. Your *target point* (best result you might achieve) — Is your *aspiration level* high enough? Never commence a negotiation until you have mentally solidified your ultimate goal with respect to *each item* to be negotiated:

3. Your estimate of *opponent's minimum settlement point* (what external options appear to be available to opponent):

4. Your estimate of *opponent's target point* (try to use his/her value system when estimating opponent's target point instead of using your own value system):

5. Your *factual and legal leverage* with respect to each issue (strengths and weaknesses of case) — Prepare logical explanations supporting each strength and anticipate ways in which you might minimize your weaknesses. Prepare rational explanations to support each component of opening position (*i.e.*,

prepare *"principled opening offer"*):

6.   Your ***opponent's factual and legal leverage*** regarding each issue (prepare effective counter-arguments):

7.   What ***information*** do you plan to elicit during ***Information Stage*** to determine opponent's underlying needs, interests, and objectives? What questions do you anticipate using? (Try to begin with broad, open-ended questions):

8.   What ***information*** are you ***willing to disclose*** and how do you plan to divulge it? (Best to disclose important information in response to opponent questions) How do you plan to prevent disclosure of sensitive information (plan use of ***"Blocking Techniques"***):

9.   Your ***negotiation strategy*** (agenda and tactics) — Plan your anticipated ***concession pattern*** carefully to disclose only the information you intend to divulge and prepare ***principled explanations*** for each planned concession:

10.   Your prediction of ***opponent's negotiation strategy*** and your planned ***Counter- measures*** — You may be able to neutralize opponent's strengths and emphasize his/her weaknesses:

11.   What ***negotiating techniques*** do you plan to use to advance your interests? (Be prepared to vary them and to combine them for optimal impact):

12. *Negotiating techniques* you expect your *opponent* will use, and way you plan to counter those actions:

II. PRELIMINARY STAGE (ESTABLISHING NEGOTIATOR IDENTITIES AND TONE FOR THE INTERACTION)

Lawyers who have previously interacted at the bargaining table are usually familiar with each other's negotiating styles. They are generally able to commence new negotiations without having to formally establish preliminary ground rules. Nonetheless, they should still take the time to reestablish rapport and cordial environments that will contribute positively to their impending discussions. Individuals who have not had extensive prior dealings with one another should expect to spend the initial portion of their interaction establishing their personal relationships, professional identities, and the tone for their subsequent discussions.

During the preliminary portion of bargaining interactions, lawyers should look for common interests they share with opponents. They may be from the same city or state, they attended the same college or law school, their children attend the same schools, they enjoy the same music or sports, etc. Persons who can identify and share such common interests enhance the probability they will like each other and develop mutually beneficial relationships.[24]

Attorneys who are unfamiliar with the negotiating styles of opposing counsel should try to obtain pre-negotiation information from other people in their own offices and from other lawyers they know. Can they expect their opponents to behave in an open and cooperative manner in which they seek to achieve mutually beneficial results or in a closed and adversarial fashion in which they try to maximize their own side's results?[25] Can they anticipate candor or dissembling from those persons? What types of bargaining techniques can they expect the other side to employ?[26]

Attorneys who encounter seemingly cooperative opponents should try to determine whether those people's apparent predisposition toward cooperative interactions is consistent with their actual behavior. Is their own openness being reciprocated by opponent candor? Until they verify this fact, they should not disclose excessive amounts of critical information regarding their own situations. They might otherwise permit manipulative adversaries to create false impressions of cooperation, so they can take advantage of one-sided disclosures by this side.[27] If lawyers find that

---

[24] *See* Christopher W. Moore, The Mediation Process 184–85 (3d ed. 2003).

[25] *See* Charles B. Craver, *Negotiation Styles: The Impact on Bargaining Transactions*, Disp. Res. J. 48 (Feb.-Apr. 2003). These are discussed in Chapter 4, *infra*.

[26] *See generally* Charles B. Craver, *Frequently Employed Negotiation Techniques*, 4 Corp. Counsel's Q. 66 (1988).

[27] *See* Gary T. Lowenthal, *A General Theory of Negotiation Process, Strategy, and Behavior*, 31 Kan. L. Rev. 69, 82 (1982).

their preliminary openness is not being reciprocated by their opponents, they should be less forthcoming with their own important information to avoid exploitation by opportunist adversaries.

As lawyers begin the Preliminary Stage, they should take the time to develop some rapport with opposing counsel. Through warm eye contact and a pleasant demeanor, they can establish a mutually supportable environment. This reduces the unproductive anxiety created by adversarial conduct. Negotiators should recognize that they can be forceful advocates without resorting to disagreeable tactics.[28] Individuals who equate offensive behavior with effective negotiating strategy will be doubly disappointed — their professional interactions will be increasingly unpleasant and they will find it more difficult to obtain optimal results for their clients.

The preliminary portion of bargaining encounters is critical, because the participants create the atmosphere that affects their entire bargaining transaction. Studies have found that persons who commence interactions in positive moods negotiate more cooperatively, share more information, are more trusting of others, and are more likely to use problem-solving efforts designed to maximize the joint returns achieved by the participants.[29] On the other hand, people who begin their encounters in negative moods negotiate more adversarially and tend to generate less efficient results. In addition, negative mood participants are more likely to resort to deceptive tactics than others, while positive mood actors are more likely to honor the agreements reached than their negative mood cohorts.[30]

Attorneys who encounter overtly competitive "win-lose" opponents should recognize that while they may not be able to convert those individuals into cooperative "win-win" negotiators, they may be able to diminish the competitive tendencies of those persons. Through friendly introductions, sincere smiles, and warm handshakes, they can try to establish more personal relationships. They can use a prolonged Preliminary Stage to enhance the negotiating atmosphere. They can attempt to sit in cooperative, rather than competitive, configurations. They can ask these opponents about their families or their colleagues, while making similar disclosures about themselves. If they can establish first-name relationships, they can accentuate the personal nature of the impending interactions.

If their preliminary efforts do not diminish the competitive behavior of opponents, lawyers may employ *"attitudinal bargaining"* to encourage more pleasant conduct.[31] They may indicate their unwillingness to view the bargaining process as a combative exercise, and suggest the need to establish some preliminary ground rules

---

[28] *See* BOB WOOLF, FRIENDLY PERSUASION 34–35 (1990). *See generally* RONALD M. SHAPIRO & MARK A. JANKOWSKI, THE POWER OF NICE (rev. ed. 2001).

[29] *See* R. Lount, *The Impact of Positive Mood on Trust in Interpersonal and Intergroup Interactions,* 98 J. PERSONALITY & SOC. PSYCH. 420, 421–22 (2010); Clark Freshman, Adele Hayes & Greg Feldman, *The Lawyer-Negotiator as Mood Scientist: What We Know and Don't Know About How Mood Relates to Successful Negotiation,* 2002 J. DISP. RES. 13, 15 (2002); Leigh L. Thompson, Janice Nadler & Peter H. Kim, *Some Like It Hot: The Case for the Emotional Negotiator, in* SHARED COGNITION IN ORGANIZATIONS: THE MANAGEMENT OF KNOWLEDGE 142–44 (Leigh L. Thompson, John M. Levine & David M. Messick, eds., 1999); Joseph P. Forgas, *On Feeling Good and Getting Your Way: Mood Effects on Negotiator Cognition and Bargaining Strategies,* 74 J. PERSONALITY & SOC. PSYCH. 565, 566–74 (1999).

[30] *See* Freshman, Hayes & Feldman, *supra* note 29, at 22-24; Thompson, Nadler & Kim, *supra* note 29, at 142–44.

[31] *See* RAIFFA, *supra* note 6, at 300-01. *See generally* WILLIAM URY, THE POWER OF A POSITIVE NO (2007); WILLIAM URY, GETTING PAST NO (1991).

for the interaction.[32] Litigators can suggest that if the other side prefers open hostility, a trial setting would be the appropriate forum due to the presence of a presiding official. Transactional negotiators may indicate that their clients are looking for mutually beneficial, on-going relationships that cannot be created and maintained through untrusting adversarial behavior.

When attitudinal bargaining fails to generate appropriate conduct, individuals who must interact with unpleasant opponents should try to control their encounters in ways that diminish the ability of offensive participants to bother them. For example, against a sarcastic and belittling opponent, they could use the telephone to conduct their discussions. When the other side's behavior begins to bother them, they can indicate that they have another call and break off talks. They can call back their adversary once they have calmed down.

III. INFORMATION STAGE (VALUE CREATION)

Once the negotiators have established their identities and the tone for their interaction, the first substantive stage of the process begins. Lawyers can easily observe the commencement of the Information Stage, because this point coincides with a shift from small talk to questions regarding the other side's needs and interests. During this part of the process, the participants work to determine the items available for joint distribution. They hope to discern the underlying interests and objectives of the other party. Proficient bargainers also look for ways to expand the overall pie to be divided, recognizing that in most situations the parties do not value each of the items identically and oppositely. The more effectively the participants can expand the pie, the more efficiently they should be able to conclude their interaction.[33]

A. Use of Information-Seeking Questions

The optimal way to elicit information from opponents is to *ask questions*.[34] During the preliminary part of the Information Stage, many parties make the mistake of asking narrow questions that can be answered with brief responses. As a result, they merely confirm what they already know. It is more effective to ask broad, open-ended information seeking questions that induce opponents to speak.[35] The more their opponents talk, the more information they directly and indirectly disclose. Lawyers who suspect something about a particular area should formulate several expansive inquiries pertaining to that area. The people being questioned usually assume that the askers know more about their side's circumstances than they actually do, and they tend to over answer the questions being asked, providing more information than they would have in response to specific questions. Only after negotiators have obtained a significant amount of information should they begin to narrow their inquiries to

---

[32] *See* HENRY S. KRAMER, GAME, SET, MATCH: WINNING THE NEGOTIATIONS GAME 264–65 (2001); LEIGH STEINBERG, WINNING WITH INTEGRITY 144–49 (1998). *See generally* URY, THE POWER OF A POSITIVE NO, *supra* note 31 and URY, GETTING PAST NO, *supra* note 31.

[33] *See* ROBERT H. MNOOKIN, SCOTT R. PEPPET & ANDREW TULUMELLO, BEYOND WINNING: NEGOTIATING TO CREATE VALUE IN DEALS AND DISPUTES 11-43 (2000).

[34] *See* JESWALD W. SALACUSE, THE GLOBAL NEGOTIATOR 48-52 (2003); LEIGH THOMPSON, THE MIND AND HEART OF THE NEGOTIATOR 60–61 (1998).

[35] *See* RUSSELL KOROBKIN, NEGOTIATION THEORY AND PRACTICE 12–13 (2002); ABRAHAM P. ORDOVER & ANDREA DONEFF, ALTERNATIVES TO LITIGATION 20–22 (2002); JOHN ILICH, DEALBREAKERS AND BREAKTHROUGHS 68 (1992).

confirm what they think they have heard.[36] If opponents attempt to avoid direct responses to these questions, to prevent the disclosure of particular information, the questioners should reframe their inquiries in a way that compels definitive replies.[37]

Skilled negotiators actively listen and carefully observe opponents during the Information Stage.[38] They maintain supportive eye contact to encourage further opponent disclosures and to discern verbal leaks and nonverbal clues. They use smiles and occasional head nods to encourage additional responses from adversaries who feel they are being heard. Active listeners not only hear what is being said, but recognize what is not being discussed, since they understand that omitted topics may suggest weaknesses opponents do not wish to address.[39]

Questioners should listen carefully for **verbal leaks** that inadvertently disclose important valuation information. For example, an opponent might say: "I **have to have** Item A, I **really want** Item B, and I would **like to get** Item C." Item A is **essential** — she has to have it. Item B is **important** — she really wants it, but does not have to have it. Item C is **desirable** — she would like to get it, but would be willing to give it up for anything better. These leaks disclose the true priorities of the items being discussed.

Advocates should proceed slowly during the Information Stage, because it takes time for the persons being questioned to decide what should be disclosed and when it should be divulged. Patient questioning and active listening are usually rewarded with the attainment of greater knowledge. Too many negotiators rush through the Information Stage, because they can hardly wait to begin the distributive portion of interactions.[40] When impatient bargainers conduct an abbreviated Information Stage, they usually miss important pieces of information and achieve agreements that are less beneficial than the accords they might have obtained through a more deliberate questioning process.

Since negotiators cannot impose their will on opponents, they must ascertain the underlying needs and interests of those parties and seek to at least minimally satisfy the basic goals of those participants. Through patient and strategically planned questioning, they can try to learn as much as possible about opponent interests, objectives, and relative preferences. What issues would the other side like to have addressed, and which terms are essential, important, and desirable? Which items do both sides consider essential or important, and which are complementary terms that can be exchanged in ways that simultaneously advance the goals of both parties?

B. Benefits of Inducing Opponents to Make First Offers

Which side should make the initial offer, and does it make any difference who goes first? Some negotiators prefer to make the first offer because they think this approach allows them to **anchor** the bargaining range and discourage wholly unrealistic opponent offers.[41] Even individuals who often go first recognize the risks

---

[36] *See* Thomas F. Guernsey, A Practical Guide to Negotiation 62–63 (1996).

[37] *See* Donald G. Gifford, Legal Negotiation: Theory and Applications 102–04 (2d ed. 2007).

[38] *See* Ordover & Doneff, *supra* note 35, at 23–26; Shapiro & Jankowsli, *supra* note 28, at 76–77; Daniel Goleman, Working with Emotional Intelligence 178–80 (1998).

[39] *See* Kramer, *supra* note 32, at 234.

[40] *See* Mark McCormack, What They Don't Teach You at Harvard Business School 152 (1984).

[41] *See* Steinberg, *supra* note 32 at 52–53; Freund, *supra* note 21, at 114–15.

of making the initial offer if they are not certain of the value of the items being exchanged. The use of preemptive first offers can be an effective technique when both sides have a realistic understanding of the items involved and have established a trusting relationship. When such factors are not present, however, I prefer to elicit first offers from my opponents for three reasons.

First, if one or both sides have miscalculated the value of the interaction, whoever goes first will disclose the misunderstanding and place themselves at a disadvantage. Even though proficient bargainers can frequently predict accurately the areas in which their adversaries will commence the process, they can never be certain. Their opponents may have over-estimated this side's strengths or over-estimated their own weaknesses, and their preliminary offer is likely to disclose this error.

A second reason to elicit first offers from the other side concerns a phenomenon known as *"bracketing."* If negotiators can induce their opponents to make the initial offers, they can *bracket* their goals by adjusting their own opening offers to keep their objectives near the mid-point between their respective opening positions.[42] For example, if plaintiff attorneys hope to obtain $500,000 and defense counsel initially offer them $250,000, they can begin with a demand of $750,000 to keep their $500,000 target in the middle. Since parties tend to move toward the center of their opening positions, due to the accepted obligation of bargaining parties to make reciprocal concessions, the people who go second can manipulate the central point and place their adversaries at a psychological disadvantage.

The third reason to induce opponents to make the initial offers concerns the fact that negotiators who make the first concessions tend to do less well than their adversaries.[43] People who make the first concessions tend to be anxious negotiators who make more and larger concessions than their opponents. Individuals who induce their adversaries to make the first offers have a good chance of persuading them the make the initial concessions. After their opponents make the initial offer, this side's opening position looks like a counter-offer. It is thus easy for this side to look to the other side for the first concession.

It is not always easy to induce opponents to make the opening offers. In some situations, the usual business practices suggest that the party initiating the bargaining encounter should begin the substantive discussions. For example, someone who has decided to sell her business may be expected to propose a price, and a person initiating a law suit may be expected to indicate what he wishes to obtain.[44] Despite this factor, skilled bargainers who might otherwise be expected to initiate the process may be able to induce less proficient opponents to do so. They may prolong the Preliminary Stage discussions and the early portions of the Information Stage until a less patient adversary simply articulates the first offer to get the substantive talks moving. These persons might alternatively begin the Information Stage by asking the opponent a number of questions that lead to a request for an opening position statement.

---

[42] *See* DAWSON, *supra* note 13, at 124-25; Richard Birke & Craig R.Fox, *Psychological Principles in Negotiating Civil Settlements*, 4 HARV. NEGOT. L. REV. 1, 41 (1999).

[43] *See* ROBERT M. BASTRESS & JOSEPH D. HARBAUGH, INTERVIEWING, COUNSELING, AND NEGOTIATING 493 (1990); HERBERT KRITZER, LET'S MAKE A DEAL 68 (1991).

[44] *See* ILICH, *supra* note 35, at 169.

Negotiators should be careful not to accept opening offers articulated by their opponents.[45] They should always respond with counteroffers of their own and allow the usual give-and-take to unfold. Even when they think opponent offers are great, they should try to talk those persons up or down a little before they accept their proposed terms. This allows their adversaries to believe that their bargaining efforts influenced the outcome, and it leaves them with the sense they obtained good deals. They might otherwise develop "buyer's remorse" and try to get out of what they now believe are bad deals.

C. Multiple Item Negotiations

When numerous terms have to be negotiated, the participants have to ascertain the degree to which each side values each item. They often obtain this information from the way in which the serious discussions commence. It is unwieldy to bargain over twenty-five or fifty items simultaneously. As a result, most negotiators begin the real talks with a group of four or five terms. They generally begin with a group of either important or unimportant items. Anxious bargainers tend to start with a group of important items, thinking that if agreement can be reached on these terms the remaining issues should be resolvable. While this is true, it is also risky. When parties begin the substantive talks by focusing on the more important items, they often reach a quick impasse. The gap between the stated positions may seem immense, and the participants may conclude that no accord is possible. On the other hand, if parties begin with a discussion of the less significant terms, they can quickly achieve tentative agreements with respect to many of the issues to be addressed. As they reach agreement on twenty then forty and even sixty percent of the items to be covered, they emphasize the areas for joint gain and become psychologically committed to settlement.[46] As they approach the more controverted terms, they remember the success they have already achieved and do not want to allow the remaining items to prevent an overall accord.[47] In addition, the final items no longer seem as insurmountable as they would have if the parties had begun their discussions with those terms.

D. How to Disclose and Withhold Important Information

While individuals prepare for a negotiation, they must decide several things regarding their own side's information. What information are they willing to disclose, and how do they plan to divulge it? What sensitive information do they wish to withhold, and how do they plan to avoid the disclosure of these facts? People who resolve these crucial issues *before* they begin to interact with their opponents are more likely to have successful Information Stages than those persons who do not think about these issues until they are forced to do so during the actual negotiations.

Negotiators who readily volunteer their critical information may encounter difficulties. As they naively disclose their interests and objectives, their statements may not be heard by opponents who are not listening intently to such statements. In addition, when adversaries do hear the information being disclosed, they tend to

---

[45] See Dawson, *supra* note 13, at 26-31.

[46] *See* Michael Watkins & Susan Rosegrant, Breakthrough International Negotiation 21–22 (2001).

[47] *See* Chester Karrass, The Negotiating Game 72–73 (1970).

discredit it because of *"reactive devaluation."*[48] They assume the disclosures are manipulative and self-serving, and they discount much of what they hear.

Bargainers who want their important information to be heard and respected should disclose that information slowly in response to opponent questions. When they answer opponent inquiries with such disclosures, their adversaries hear more of what they are saying because people listen more intently to the answers to their own questions. In addition, opponents attribute these disclosures to their question capabilities and accord what they hear greater respect.

What should negotiators do when opponents ask them about areas they would prefer not to address? They should appreciate the fact that it is much easier to avoid the disclosure of important information if their adversaries are unaware of the fact that knowledge is being withheld. The most effective way to accomplish this objective is through the use of *"blocking techniques."*[49] These tactics are regularly employed by politicians who do not wish to provide answers to sensitive questions that may cost them votes no matter how they respond. People who listen carefully to such politicians will be amazed by the number of inquiries that go unanswered.

The first blocking technique involves ignoring the question being asked. Negotiators who do not like a particular inquiry should continue the current conversation or change the discussion to other topics they would prefer to explore as if they never heard the question that was propounded. If they can get their opponents caught up in their continued talks, those persons may forget to restate their initial inquiry.

Someone being asked a three or four part question can focus on the part she likes and ignore the rest. If she can induce her opponent to focus on the part being addressed, he may never return to the other parts of the initial inquiry. A person being asked a delicate question may over or under answer it. If he is asked a specific question, he can provide a general response. If asked a general inquiry, he can give a narrow response. He might alternatively misinterpret the question being asked. An opponent asks about a particular topic, and he responds by indicating that the opponent must be concerned about a different subject. He then steers the discussion in the direction he would like to see it progress. If he can induce his adversary to focus on the new area being discussed, that person may fail to restate the original inquiry.

Questions occasionally seek information of a confidential or privileged nature. The person asking these questions hopes to catch the respondent off guard and induce that person to provide an answer. When negotiators commence bargaining interactions, they should determine what information they are not willing to disclose. What information concerns confidential lawyer-client communications? What information is privileged (*e.g.*, attorney work product)? They should be prepared to respond to opponent inquiries pertaining to these areas by indicating that they concern confidential or privileged matters they are not willing to discuss. Once adversaries realize they are not going to answer these questions, those persons will move on to other areas.

---

[48] *See* MNOOKIN, PEPPET & TULUMELLO, *supra* note 33, at 165.

[49] *See* BASTRESS & HARBAUGH, *supra* note 43, at 422–28; FREUND, *supra* note 21, at 64–65.

E. Exploring Underlying Needs and Interests of Parties

When an expansive settlement range exists between the bottom lines of the two sides, the participants should be able to achieve accords. Their resulting agreement, however, will probably not be a Pareto superior solution — where neither party could enhance its present circumstances without simultaneously worsening the other side's situation. If the parties can thoughtfully explore their respective underlying interests and rely upon objective standards to guide their discussions, they should be able to expand the overall pie and enhance the benefits to both sides.[50]

Although many legal practitioners consider the negotiation process an inherently adversarial endeavor, they should appreciate the benefits that may be derived during the Information Stage from the use of non-adversarial questioning techniques. Too many bargainers make the mistake of assuming that the parties have a fixed amount of goods to be divided — *i.e.*, identical value systems and analogous utility functions that generate zero-sum transactions.[51] If they replaced leading questions, intended to challenge the positions being taken by opponents, with more neutral questions designed to elicit the underlying needs and interests of the other side, the negotiators could more easily look for areas that would allow joint gains.[52]

Even entirely monetary transactions do not have to be regarded as zero-sum endeavors. The two sides may have quite different preference curves with respect to the value of money. In addition, through the use of in-kind payments consisting of goods or services, the parties may convert their interaction into a non-zero-sum transaction. A purchaser of a company may agree to provide $50 million in cash and $15 million in goods or services. The seller believes she just sold her firm for $65 million, while the purchaser thinks he only paid $59 million, because it only cost $9 million to generate the goods and services valued by the seller for $15 million. The parties may alternatively provide for some future payments that may be considered beneficial by both sides.

People involved with multi-item negotiations must appreciate the fact that the parties probably value the various items quite differently. This enables them to look for exchanges that can simultaneously benefit both sides.[53] For example, individuals negotiating the terms for a marital dissolution may be discussing their primary residence and vacation home, their SUV and sports car, custody of their two young children, child support payments, and possible alimony. They may be arguing over joint custody, when only one spouse really wants primary parenting responsibilities. If the spouse who does not strongly desire primary parenting obligations is provided with adequate visitation rights, he or she may provide the other person with the primary residence in which to continue living with the children and the SUV needed

---

[50] The use of integrative bargaining techniques to maximize the joint returns achieved by the negotiating parties will be discussed in connection with the Cooperative Stage, *infra*. If the parties fail to explore their underlying interests and needs during the Information Stage, it makes it less likely that they will be able to make the exchanges during the subsequent Cooperative Stage that will generate efficient results.

[51] *See* Birke & Fox, *supra* note 42, at 30–31; James J.Gillespie, Leigh L. Thompson, Jeffrey Loewenstein & Dedre Gentner, *Lessons from Analogical Reasoning in the Teaching of Negotiation*, 15 Negot. J. 363, 367 (1999).

[52] *See* Raiffa, *supra* note 6, at 198–201; Mnookin, Peppet & Tulumello, *supra* note 33, at 11-44; Carrie Menkel-Meadow, *Toward Another View of Legal Negotiation: The Structure of Problem Solving*, 31 U.C.L.A. L. Rev. 754, 813 (1984); Fisher & Ury *supra* note 5, at 41–57.

[53] *See* Shapiro & Jankowsli, *supra* note 28, at 101-03; Michael Watkins, *Principles of Persuasion*, 17 Negot. J. 115, 124 (2001).

to transport the children, in exchange for the vacation home and the sports car. They can then talk about child support payments and possible alimony.

If negotiators hope to expand the overall pie and ultimately explore beneficial exchanges that may simultaneously benefit both sides, they must initially classify the goals sought by their respective sides as "essential," "important," and "desirable." They must then endeavor to determine during their information exchanges the degree to which their own side's goals conflict with the objectives of the other side.[54] In some instances, both parties may actually desire the identical distribution of the items in question ("shared needs"), allowing them to enhance their respective interests at the same time. In other situations, each may wish to attain independent objectives that do not conflict with the interests of their opponent ("independent needs"). In only some areas do both parties wish to claim the identical items for themselves. Even with respect to these "conflicting needs" the two sides must ascertain the degree to which each prefers the terms in question. One may consider them "essential," while the other may only regard them as "important" or "desirable." The party with a higher preference should be willing to trade terms of lesser value to obtain the items they prefer to get. Only when the parties both value conflicting needs identically are both going to vie for them. In these areas, even trades of similarly valued terms can move the parties toward final accords.

IV. DISTRIBUTIVE STAGE (VALUE CLAIMING)

The transition from the Information Stage to the Distributive Stage is usually visible. The participants cease asking each other what they want and why they want it, and begin to talk about what they have to have or are willing to give up. During the Information Stage the focus is primarily upon *opponents*, as the negotiators try to ascertain what is available for distribution and determine the degree to which the other party values the items to be exchanged. During the Distributive Stage, the focus is on our *own sides* as we — and our adversaries — begin to claim the items we discovered during the previous stage.

No matter how much altruistic negotiators try to create win-win bargaining environments, there will always be items both sides wish to obtain. Most proficient legal representatives hope to claim more of the conflicted terms for their own clients. In their book *The Power of Nice*, Ron Shapiro and Mark Jankowski unambiguously articulate this philosophy: "[W]e're out to achieve *all* (or most) of *our* goals, to make *our most desirable deal*. But the best way to do so is to let the other side achieve *some* of *their* goals, to make their acceptable deal. That's **WIN-win**: big win for your side, little win for theirs."[55] Throughout the Distributive Stage, the parties compete for these mutually desired terms.[56]

---

[54] *See* RAIFFA, *supra* note 6, at 199-201; WATKINS & ROSEGRANT, *supra* note 46, at 22–23; Carrie Menkel-Meadow, *Aha? Is Creativity Possible in Legal Problem Solving and Teachable in Legal Education?* 6 HARV. NEGOT. L. REV. 97, 109–111 (2001).

[55] SHAPIRO & JANKOWSKI, *supra* note 28, at 5 (emphasis in original).

[56] *See* Charles B. Craver, *The Inherent Tension Between Value Creation and Value Claiming During Bargaining Interactions*, 12 CARDOZO J. CONFLICT RES. 1 (2010).

A.   Carefully Planned Concession Patterns

Persuasive bargainers begin the Distributive Stage with the articulation of "principled" positions that rationally explain why they deserve what they are offering or seeking. This bolsters their confidence in their own positions, and undermines the confidence of less prepared opponents in their own positions. Proficient negotiators also begin with carefully prepared concession patterns.[57] They know how they plan to move from their opening offers to their final objectives. They may intend to make several deliberate, but expansive, concessions, or prefer to employ a series of incremental position changes. They know that this aspect of their strategy must be thoughtfully choreographed to maximize their bargaining effectiveness. They try to make only *"principled concessions"* that they can rationally explain to their adversaries. This lets others know why they are making the precise position change being articulated, and indicates why a greater modification is not presently warranted. This approach also helps them to remain at their new position until they obtain a reciprocal concession from the other side.

The timing of concessions is important. Many anxious negotiators find it difficult to cope with the uncertainty indigenous to the bargaining process, and they often make rapid — and occasionally unreciprocated — concessions in a desperate effort to generate accords. They ignore the fact that 80 percent of position changes tend to occur during the last 20 percent of interactions.[58] People who attempt to expedite transactions in an artificial manner usually pay a high price for their impatience.[59]

Concessions must be carefully formulated and tactically announced. If properly used, a position change can signal a cooperative attitude; it can also communicate the need for a counteroffer if the opponent intends to continue the bargaining process. If carelessly issued, however, a concession can signal anxiety and a loss of control. This may occur when a position change is announced in a tentative and unprincipled manner by an individual who continues to talk nervously and defensively after the concession has been articulated. Such behavior suggests that the speaker does not expect immediate reciprocity from the other side. When one encounters such individuals, they should subtly encourage them to keep talking, since this approach may generate additional, unanswered concessions.[60] To avoid this problem, proficient negotiators announce their position changes with appropriate explanations, then shift the focus to their opponents. By exuding a patient silence at this point, they indicate that reciprocal behavior must be forthcoming if the interaction is to continue.

The exact amount and precise timing of each position change are critical. Each successive concession should be smaller than the preceding one, and each should normally be made in response to an appropriate counteroffer from the opponent. If a subsequent change is greater than the prior ones, this may signal that the conceding party is adrift. If successive concessions are made too quickly, this may similarly indicate a lack of control. Following each change, the focus should be shifted to the other side. Patient silence will let the other party know that they must reciprocate to keep the process moving.[61]

---

[57] *See* FREUND, *supra* note 21, at 130-41.

[58] *See* DAWSON, *supra* note 13, at 172.

[59] *See* LePOOLE, *supra* note 8, at 72.

[60] *See* John C. Harsanyi, *Bargaining and Conflict Situations in Light of a New Approach to Game Theory, in* BARGAINING: FORMAL THEORIES OF NEGOTIATION 74, 80–81 (Oran R. Young, ed., 1975).

[61] *See* PRATKANIS & ARONSON, *supra* note 23, at 180-81.

Although negotiators should carefully plan their concession patterns in advance, they must remain flexible in recognition of the fact that opponents do not always react to position changes as initially expected. Participants must thus be prepared to change their planned behavior as new information regarding adversary strengths, weaknesses, and preferences is obtained.[62] They should not only be prepared to adjust their aspiration level, when appropriate, but also be ready to alter their concession strategy based upon mutually acknowledged objective criteria.[63] They must be patient, recognizing that a particular interaction may take longer to complete than they originally anticipated. When concessions are small and the issues are numerous and/or complex, negotiators must allow the process to develop deliberately. If they try to hasten the transaction in an unnatural way, they may place themselves at a tactical disadvantage.[64]

Negotiators should always remember their nonsettlement options and preliminarily established resistence points as they approach their bottom lines during bargaining interactions. They must recognize the fact that it would be irrational to accept proposed terms that are less beneficial than their external alternatives. As the Distributive Stage unfolds and they approach their resistence points, many advocates feel greater pressure to settle, when they should actually feel less pressure to achieve accords. When the terms being offered by opponents are not much better than their nonsettlement options, participants approaching their bottom lines possess more — not less — bargaining power than the offerors. Such persons have little to lose if no agreements are achieved, thus they should not be afraid to reject the disadvantageous proposals on the table. Instead of exuding weakness, as many negotiators do in these circumstances, they should project strength. Since their opponents are likely to lose more than they lose from nonsettlements, they can confidently demand further concessions as a prerequisite to any final accord.

As the Distributive Stage develops, the parties frequently encounter temporary impasses. The participants are attempting to obtain optimal terms for their respective clients, and each is hoping to induce the other to make the next position change. Individuals who have viable external options should not hesitate to disclose — at least minimally — this critical fact. The more their adversaries know about these alternatives, the more likely they are to appreciate the need for more accommodating behavior. It is usually most effective to convey this information in a calm and non-confrontational manner.[65] Bargainers who refuse to divulge the scope of their nonsettlement options at critical points often fail to achieve accords that may have been attainable had their adversaries been fully aware of their actual circumstances.

Despite the competitive nature of distributive bargaining, a cooperative/problem-solving approach is more likely to produce beneficial results than a competitive/adversarial strategy.[66] The former style permits the participants to

---

[62] *See* P.H. Gulliver, Disputes and Negotiations: A Cross-Cultural Perspective 100 (1979).

[63] *See* Fisher & Ury, *supra* note 5, at 88–89.

[64] *See* Jeffrey Rubin & Bert Brown, The Social Psychology of Bargaining and Negotiation 145 (1975).

[65] *See* Freund, *supra* note 21 at 47.

[66] *See generally* Andrea Kupfer Schneider, *Shattering Negotiation Myths: Empirical Evidence on the Effectiveness of Negotiation Style*, 7 Harv. Negot. L. Rev. 143 (2002). In her empirical study of attorneys in Milwaukee and Chicago, Professor Schneider found that while 54 percent of cooperative/problem-solving lawyers were considered by their peers to be effective negotiators, only 9 percent of competitive/adversarial bargainers were viewed as effective. *Id.* at 167. On the other hand, while only 3.6 percent of cooperative/problem-solving negotiators were rated ineffective, 53.3 percent of competitive/adversarial bargainers were.

explore the opportunity for mutual gain in a relatively objective and detached manner.[67] The latter approach, however, is more likely to generate mistrust and an unwillingness of the negotiators to share sensitive information.

When specific offers are met with unreceptive responses, negotiators can employ their questioning skills to direct the attention of opponents toward the areas that may generate joint gains. This may enable them to elicit information from their adversaries regarding their underlying interests and goals.[68] As they obtain helpful insights pertaining to the other side's value system, they should divulge information concerning their own side's objectives. This approach may permit the parties to generate a minimal degree of trust and encourage the participants to employ a problem-solving approach.

During this part of the negotiation process, participants should listen carefully for *verbal leaks* that subtly indicate that the other side is actually willing to modify its current position. For example, she might say "I ***don't want*** to go higher" or "I'm ***not inclined*** to go higher." The verbal leaks "don't want" and "not inclined" strongly suggest that if her opponent is patient, the speaker will increase her offer.

No matter how effectively negotiators have been interacting, they occasionally find themselves moving toward an impasse. Before they permit an impending stalemate to preclude further talks, they should consider other options that may enable them to keep the process moving.[69] They may reframe especially emotional issues in an effort to find more neutral language that may be more acceptable to both sides. They may temporarily change the focus of their discussions, ceasing to talk about the issues on which they have been concentrating and moving to other issues that may regenerate stalled discussions. They may briefly talk about recent political events, sports, weather, mutual acquaintances, or similar topics, hoping to relieve their bargaining tension. It can be helpful to recount a humorous story that will humanize the participants and remind them not to take the current circumstances too seriously.

When the bargaining atmosphere becomes unusually tense, it may be beneficial for the parties to take a break to allow themselves to cool off and reconsider their positions. They should carefully review their nonsettlement alternatives and contemplate unexplored bargaining options that may enable them to expand the pie and generate better joint agreements. Before they recess the talks, however, they should set a firm date for their next session. If they fail to do this, each may be hesitant to contact the other lest they appear weak.

B.   Power Bargaining

The Distributive Stage generally involves some degree of power bargaining, as the participants attempt to obtain optimal results for their respective clients concerning the items both sides value.[70] The purpose of this approach is to induce opponents to think they have to provide more generous terms than they actually have to provide. This objective may be accomplished by inducing those persons to reassess their own situations. Have operative weaknesses been ignored or inappropriately minimized? Have their strengths been over-estimated? Negotiators may expand their own power by convincing adversaries that they possess greater strength or less vulnerability

---

[67] *See* GIFFORD, *supra* note 37, at 15-18.

[68] *See* MAX H. BAZERMAN & MARGARET A. NEAL, NEGOTIATING RATIONALLY 90-95 (1992).

[69] *See* DAWSON, *supra* note 13, at 67-74.

[70] *See generally* Gerald B. Wetlaufer, *The Limits of Integrative Bargaining*, 85 GEO. L.J. 369 (1996).

than their opponents think they do.[71] They may casually mention possible nonsettlement options their opponents may not think are available to them, or suggest ways they can avoid negative consequences the other side thinks they will suffer if accords are not achieved.

Self assurance is one of the most important attributes possessed by successful negotiators. They exude an inner confidence in their positions, and always appear to be in control of the situation. They do not appear to fear the possibility of nonsettlements, suggesting to opponents that they have developed alternatives that will protect their clients if the current negotiations are unproductive. These factors cause less certain adversaries to accord these persons more power and respect than they objectively deserve.

Proficient bargainers always commence their interactions with high and well supported aspiration levels, while less skilled negotiators often begin with deflated goals, fearing that their initial demands may engender hostility if they are not modest. The confidence exhibited by the more prepared negotiators with higher aspirations frequently causes less prepared bargainers with lower goals to doubt the propriety of their minimal objectives. They assume the high goal participants possess beneficial nonsettlement alternatives, and accord them greater respect than they deserve.

C. Common Power Bargaining Tactics

During the Distributive Stage, the participants employ various techniques to advance their interests. Some are used in isolation, while others are employed simultaneously. These tactics are generally designed to keep opponents off balance and to induce them to think they have to make greater concessions if the bargaining process is to continue. Negotiators should carefully plan their own techniques, and anticipate and prepare for the tactics they think the other side will use.

(1) *Argument*

The negotiating tactic employed most frequently by lawyers involves legal and nonlegal argument.[72] When the facts support their positions, they emphasize the factual aspects of the transaction. When legal doctrines support their claim, they cite statutes, regulations, judicial decisions, and scholarly publications. Public policy may be cited when it advances client positions. When appropriate, economic and/or political considerations will be used.

Negotiators do not really use arguments to elucidate, but rather to convince opponents to give them what they wish to achieve.[73] Persuasive advocates are persons who are able to provide adversaries with seemingly valid reasons to provide them with their objectives. They employ apparently objective standards to bolster their claims. They also frame the issues to be resolved in ways that lend moral support to their own positions.[74] Individuals with greater bargaining power tend to argue in

---

[71] *See* SAMUEL B. BACHARACH & EDWARD J. LAWLER, BARGAINING: POWER, TACTICS AND OUTCOMES 60–63 (1981).

[72] *See* Gerald WILLIAMS, LEGAL NEGOTIATION AND SETTLEMENT 79–81 (1983).

[73] *See* Robert Condlin, *Cases on Both Sides: Patterns of Argument in Legal Dispute-Negotiation*, 44 MD. L. REV. 65, 73 (1985).

[74] *See* SHELL, *supra* note 15, at 104-05.

favor of equitable distributions that favor their own side, while persons with less power tend to argue for egalitarian distributions.[75]

Persuasive arguments have to be presented in a relatively even-handed and objective manner if they are to appeal to opposing parties.[76] They are most effective when presented in a logical and orderly sequence that will have a cumulative impact upon the recipients. Instead of merely restating arguments, speakers should restate them in different forms that are designed to enhance their persuasiveness.

Proficient bargainers work to develop innovative arguments they hope have not been anticipated by opponents. Once adversaries are forced to internally question their previously developed rationales supporting their own positions, they begin to suffer a loss of bargaining confidence. The weakening of their underlying positional foundations causes them to seriously consider the legal and factual interpretations being offered by their adversaries.

Lawyers should not ignore the potential persuasiveness of well-crafted emotional appeals.[77] While most attorneys are intelligent people who can easily counter logical assertions, they often find it difficult to ignore emotional presentations that generate guilt or compassion. Advocates should thus formulate arguments that are designed to elicit emotional responses, because these appeals may produce beneficial results.

(2) *Threats, Warnings, and Promises*

Almost all legal negotiations involve the use of overt or implicit threats. Transactional negotiators indicate that they will deal with other parties if this side does not sweeten its offer, while litigators suggest that they will resort to adjudications if they do not get what they want at the bargaining table. Threats are employed to convince opponents that the cost of disagreeing with proposed offers transcends the cost of acquiescence.[78]

Less confrontational negotiators try to avoid the use of direct "*threats*," preferring to use less challenging "*warnings*." Instead of threatening to personally impose negative consequences on their opponents if they do not change their positions, these people caution their adversaries about the consequences that will naturally result from their failure to accept mutual accords.[79] These "warnings" do not concern action that the declarants plan to take, but events that will independently evolve if no settlements are achieved. The negative effects may be imposed by absent clients, judges, or the market place.

When adverse consequences are likely to occur, it is usually beneficial to articulate the negative possibilities as "warnings" rather than "threats."[80] Threats are direct affronts to opponents and often induce reciprocal behavior; warnings are more indirect, based on what a third party will do, making such warnings more palatable to listeners.[81] In addition, the warning device enhances the credibility of the negative

---

[75] *See* BIRKE & FOX, *supra* note 42, at 34–35.

[76] *See* Bastress & Harbaugh, *supra* note 43, at 437–38.

[77] *See id.* at 439–40.

[78] *See* Thomas C. Schelling, *An Essay on Bargaining, in* BARGAINING: FORMAL THEORIES OF NEGOTIATION 319, 329–34 (Oran R. Young, ed., 1975).

[79] *See* FREUND, *supra* note 21, at 212-13; FRED C. IKLE, HOW NATIONS NEGOTIATE 62–63 (1964).

[80] *See* Jon Elster, *Strategic Uses of Argument, in* BARRIERS TO CONFLICT RESOLUTION 236, 252–53 (Kenneth Arrow, Robert H. Mnookin, Lee Ross, Amos Tversky & Robert Wilson, eds., 1995).

[81] *See* ROBERT MAYER, POWER PLAYS 64–65 (1996).

consequences being discussed, since the speakers are suggesting that the adverse effects will result from the actions of third parties over whom they exert minimal or no control.

At the opposite end of the spectrum from negative threats and warnings are affirmative *"promises."*[82] A "promise" does not involve the suggestion of negative consequences, but rather consists of "an expressed intention to behave in a way that appears beneficial to the interests of another."[83] For example, instead of threatening legal action if an opponent does not alter her current position, a negotiator indicates that if the other side provides a more generous offer, he will respond with a better offer of his own. The affirmative promise provides a face-saving way for opposing sides to move jointly toward each other, because it promises reciprocal action in response to a change by the other party.

Threats, warnings, and promises convey significant information concerning the transmitter's perception of the opponent's circumstances. Threats and warnings disclose what the threatening side thinks the listener fears, while promises indicate what the promisor believes the recipient hopes to obtain. People given threats, warnings, or promises may be able to use these tactics to their own advantage. If, for example, if an adversary suggests through a threat or warning that she believes that this side would lose more from a nonsettlement than it would actually lose, it may be beneficial to disabuse the threatener of this misperception to prevent her from over-estimating this side's need to reach an agreement. Conversely, if the other side appears to desire a particular item for his client that is not valued by this side, an adroit negotiator can try to extract some other meaningful term in exchange for this item.

Proficient negotiators tend to transmit affirmative promises more frequently than they do negative threats or warnings.[84] This surprises many bargainers, because most people remember disruptive threats and warnings more than face-saving promises, causing them to over-estimate the number of threats and warnings they encountered. The use of promises increases the likelihood of mutual accords, while the use of threats and warnings reduces this probability.[85]

Negotiators who plan to employ threats to advance their agendas should appreciate the characteristics of effective threats. The proposed negative consequences must be carefully communicated to opponents, and the threatened result must be proportionate to the action the user is seeking. Insignificant threats are ignored as irrelevant, while excessive threats are dismissed as irrational.[86] In addition, bargainers should never issue ultimatums they are not prepared to effectuate, because if their bluffs are called and they back down, their credibility is lost.[87]

Negotiators who are threatened with negative consequences if they do not change their current positions must always consider a critical factor. What is likely to happen

---

[82] *See* DEAN G. PRUITT & JEFFREY Z. RUBIN, SOCIAL CONFLICT 51–55 (1986); Schelling, *supra* note 78, at 335–37.

[83] RUBIN & BROWN, *supra* note 64, at 278.

[84] *See id.* at 282.

[85] *See id.* at 286.

[86] *See* RICHARD NED LEBOW, THE ART OF BARGAINING 92–93 (1996); Gary T. Lowenthal, *A General Theory of Negotiaiton Process, Strategy, and Behavior*, 31 KAN. L. REV. 69, 86 (1982).

[87] *See* LEBOW, *supra* note 86, at 107; MAYER, *supra* note 81, at 64.

to their side if no agreement is reached with the other side? If their external alternatives are preferable to what would be the result if they acceded to their opponent's threat, these persons should not be afraid to maintain their present positions. If they wish to preserve a positive bargaining atmosphere, hoping that continued discussions will cause their adversaries to move in their direction, they can simply ignore the threat.[88] If threatened parties behave as if no ultimatum has been issued, the other side may be able to withdraw the threat without suffering a loss of face.

(3) *Ridicule and Humor*

Humor can be used by people during the Preliminary Stage of the bargaining process to help them create more positive environments. Studies indicate that the use of humor can increase the likability of the communicators.[89] This approach can help negotiators develop more open and trusting relationships with opponents. Humor may also be employed during the Distributive Stage to induce adversaries to accept proposals they might otherwise be hesitant to accept.[90] When negotiations become unusually tense, a one-liner can remind the other side that the parties should not be taking the situation so seriously.

Ridicule and humor can be employed by negotiators to indicate negative responses to poor proposals. For example, a derisive smile or sarcastic laughter may be used in response to an especially one-sided offer to demonstrate how unacceptable it is. If employed skillfully, this approach may embarrass an opponent and induce that person to make another more reasonable offer. If used less proficiently, such behavior may anger the other side and create an unproductive environment.

(4) *Silence*

Silence is an extremely effective bargaining tactic often overlooked by negotiators.[91] Less competent negotiators fear silence. They are afraid that if they stop talking, they will lose control of the interaction. They remember the awkwardness they have experienced in social settings during prolonged pauses, and they feel compelled to speak. When they prattle on, they tend to disclose, both verbally and nonverbally, information they did not intend to divulge, and they frequently make unintended concessions.[92] When confronted by further silence from adversaries, they continue their verbal leakage and concomitant loss of control.

When negotiators have something important to convey, they should succinctly say what they have to say and become silent. There is no need to emphasize the point with unnecessary reiteration. They need to give their listener the chance to absorb what has been said.[93] This approach is especially critical when concessions are being exchanged. Bargainers should articulate their new positions and quietly and patiently await responses from the receiving parties. If the prolonged silence makes them feel uncomfortable, they should review their notes or look out the window. Their calm patience indicates to the other side that they expect a response before they continue the discussions.

---

[88] *See* Bastress & Harbaugh, *supra* note 43, at 461–62.

[89] *See* K. O'Quin & J. Aronoff, *Humor as a Technique of Social Influence*, 44 Soc. Psych. Q. 349 (1981).

[90] *See id.* at 354.

[91] *See* Steinberg, *supra* note 32, at 171.

[92] *See* Mark McCormack, What They Don't Teach You at Harvard Business School 108–11 (1984).

[93] *See* Mayer, *supra* note 81, at 30.

Negotiators who encounter impatient opponents who exhibit an inability to remain silent should use extended pauses to their own advantage. After talkative adversaries make position changes, they may become disconcerted if they receive no responses. As their anxiety increases, they may be induced to say more and even bid against themselves through the articulation of unreciprocated concessions.

(5) *Patience*

Persons involved in bargaining interactions must appreciate the fact the process takes time to unfold. Individuals who seek to accelerate developments usually obtain less favorable and less efficient results than they would have attained had they been more patient. Offers that would have been acceptable if conveyed during the latter stages of a negotiation may not be attractive when conveyed prematurely. The participants have not had sufficient time to appreciate the fact that a negotiated deal is preferable to their external alternatives.

All negotiators experience some anxiety created by the uncertainty that is inherent in bargaining encounters. Individuals who can control the tension they experience and exude a quiet confidence are generally able to achieve better deals than less patient persons. They exhibit a stamina that indicates that they are prepared to take as long as necessary to attain their objectives. Less patient opponents often give in, because they are unwilling to take the time they have to expend to generate better results for their own side.

Negotiators who hope to use their own stamina to wear down less patient adversaries should develop pleasant styles that help them keep the process going when circumstances become difficult. If the bargaining environment becomes unusually tense, they might use short breaks to alleviate the tension. If they can convince their opponents that they will continue the process until they achieve their goals, they will frequently obtain capitulations from less committed adversaries.

(6) *Guilt, Embarrassment, and Indebtedness*

Some negotiators seek to create feelings of guilt or embarrassment in opponents for the purpose of inducing those persons to accede to their demands. They cite insignificant transgressions, such as someone showing up late for a meeting or forgetting to bring an unimportant document, hoping to disconcert adversaries. These persons wish to make the others feel so uncomfortable that they will try to regain social acceptability by doing something nice for them. When someone tries to place a bargaining participant at a disadvantage over a small oversight, they should simply apologize and move on without feeling the need to give up something of substance.

(7) *Voice and Language*

Some negotiators are afraid to raise their voices during interactions for fear of offending opponents. They fail to appreciate the beneficial impact that can be achieved through the strategic use of loudness. Controlled voice volume can be a characteristic of persuasiveness. When individuals talk in a louder voice, others tend to listen. So long as the raised voice is not viewed as inappropriately aggressive or offensive, it does not hurt to speak more loudly when someone really wants to be heard.

Many persons think they will be more persuasive negotiators if they use more intense language during their interactions. Studies show, however, that low intensity discussions are likely to be more persuasive than high intensity presentations.[94] This seeming anomaly is due to the negative reaction most negotiators have toward high intensity persuasive efforts. High intensity speakers seem manipulative and offensive, while low intensity presenters tend to induce opponents to be less suspicious of and more receptive to their entreaties.

D. Negotiators Must Always Remember their Nonsettlement Options

Throughout the Distributive Stage, negotiators should always remember their *current nonsettlement alternatives*. It is no longer relevant what they were six months or a year ago, when these individuals began to prepare for the present interaction. The passage of time has generally affected the options that were previously available. The discovery process may have strengthened or weakened the case of litigators, while changes in the business market may have influenced the value of the transaction being discussed. Has the market improved the situation of the firm being purchased or sold? Are the technology rights being licensed worth more or less than they were a year ago?

If bargainers fail to appreciate changes in the value of the present interactions, they may enter into arrangements that are not better than what they would have had with no agreement. They must always remember that bad deals are worse than no deals.[95] When nonsettlement alternatives are presently more beneficial than the terms being offered at the bargaining table, they should not hesitate to walk away from the current discussions. They should do this as pleasantly as possible, for two reasons. First, when their opponents realize that these persons are really willing to end the interaction, their adversaries may reconsider their positions and offer them more beneficial terms.[96] Second, even if the current negotiations fail to regenerate and no accord is achieved, the parties may see each other in the future. If both parties remember these talks favorably, even if they were not successful, future negotiations are likely to progress more smoothly than if these talks ended on an unpleasant note.

V. CLOSING STAGE (VALUE SOLIDIFYING)

Near the end of the Distributive Stage, the participants realize that a mutual accord is likely to be achieved. They feel a sense of relief, because the anxiety generated by the uncertainty of the negotiation process is about to be alleviated by the attainment of a definitive agreement. Careful observers can often see signs of relief around the mouths of the negotiators, and they may exhibit more relaxed postures. As the bargainers become psychologically committed to settlement, they may move too quickly toward the conclusion of the transaction.

The Closing Stage represents a critical part of the bargaining process. The majority of concessions tend to be made during the concluding portion of negotiations,[97] and overly anxious participants may forfeit much of what they

---

[94] *See* Roy J. Lewicki, Joseph A. Litterer, John W. Minton & David M. Saunders, Negotiation 214 (2d ed. 1994).

[95] *See* Grande Lum, The Negotiation Fieldbook 54–55 (2011).

[96] *See* Dawson, *supra* note 13, at 194–98.

[97] *See id.* at 172.

obtained during the Distributive Stage if they are not careful. They must remain patient and allow the Closing Stage to develop in a deliberate fashion.

By the conclusion of the Distributive Stage, *both sides* have become psychologically committed to a joint resolution. Neither wants their prior bargaining efforts to culminate in failure. Less proficient negotiators focus almost entirely on their own side's desire for an agreement, completely disregarding the settlement pressure affecting their opponents. As the Closing Stage commences, *both sides* want an agreement. It is thus appropriate for both parties to expect joint movement toward final terms. Negotiators should be careful not to make unreciprocated concessions, and to avoid excessive position changes. They should only contemplate larger concessions than their adversaries when their opponents have been more accommodating during the earlier exchanges and the verbal and nonverbal signals emanating from those participants indicate that they are approaching their resistance points.

The Closing Stage is not a time for swift action; it is a time for ***patient perseverance***. Negotiators should continue to employ the tactics that got them to this point, and they should be well aware of their prior and present concession patterns. They should endeavor to make smaller, and, if possible, less frequent position changes than their opponents. If they fail to heed this warning and move too quickly toward a conclusion, they are likely to close most of the gap remaining between the parties.

Patience and silence are two of the most effective techniques during the Closing Stage. Negotiators should employ "principled" concessions to explain the reasons for their exact moves. Following each announced position change, they should become silent and patiently await the other side's response. They should not prattle on and disclose their anxiety, and they should not contemplate further movement without reciprocity from the other side. They must remember that their adversaries are as anxious to achieve final terms as they are.

Skilled bargainers are often able to obtain a significant advantage during the Closing Stage by exhibiting a calm indifference. If negotiators can persuade their anxious opponents that they really do not care whether final terms are achieved, their adversaries may be induced to close most of the distance remaining between the parties.[98] As those participants make more expansive and more frequent concessions in an effort to guarantee an agreement, these persons significantly enhance the terms achieved by this side.

The Closing Stage can be a highly competitive portion of the negotiation process. It often involves a substantial number of position changes and a significant amount of participant movement. Negotiators who think that this part of the interaction consists primarily of cooperative behavior are likely to obtain less beneficial results than strategic opponents who use this stage to induce naive adversaries to close more of the outstanding distance between the two sides. As they plan their closing strategies, negotiators must remember that their adversaries also wish to attain final accords. Their opponents may be even more anxious in this regard than they are. If they carefully and deliberately move toward agreement, they may induce their more anxious opponents to give them better deals than they deserve.

Negotiators who think their opponents are approaching their bottom lines should listen carefully for ***verbal leaks*** indicating that they are not. Their opponent may say "that's ***about as far*** as I can go" or "I don't have ***much more room***" — both of which

---

[98] *See id.* at 173–76.

indicate that the speaker has more room. When bargainers get to their true bottom lines, they say something like "that's as far as I can go," and they tend to have an open, palms-up posture supporting their representation that they are really at their reservation point.

VI. COOPERATIVE STAGE (VALUE MAXIMIZING)

After the Closing Stage has been successfully completed through the attainment of a mutually acceptable agreement, many persons consider the negotiation process finished. While this conclusion may be correct with respect to zero sum problems, such as the immediate exchange of money, where neither party could improve its results without a corresponding loss to the other side,[99] it is certainly not true for multi-issue encounters. Nonetheless, many participants in multi-issue bargaining assume a fixed pie that cannot be expanded.[100] This is rarely correct, due to the different client preference curves involved.[101] As a result, it is frequently possible for the negotiators to formulate proposals that may expand the pie and simultaneously advance their respective interests.

Once a tentative accord has been reached through the distributive process, the negotiators should contemplate alternative trade-offs that might concurrently enhance the interests of both parties. The bargainers may be mentally, and even physically, exhausted from their prior discussions, but they should at least briefly explore alternative formulations that may prove to be mutually advantageous. During the Information Stage, the parties often over- or under-state the actual value of different items for strategic reasons. During the Distributive and Closing Stages, they tend to be cautious and opportunistic. Both sides are likely to employ power bargaining tactics designed to achieve results favorable to their own circumstances. Because of the tension created by these distributive techniques, Pareto superior arrangements are rarely attained by this point in the negotiation process. The participants are likely to have only achieved "acceptable" terms. If they conclude their interaction at this point, they may leave a substantial amount of untapped joint satisfaction on the bargaining table.

In simulation exercises, it is easy to determine the extent to which negotiators have successfully used the Cooperative Stage. By comparing the aggregate point totals attained by the two sides, one may assess the degree to which they maximized their joint results. For example, where two opponents might potentially divide 800 points between themselves, some participants with proficient cooperative skills may reach agreements giving them combined totals of 750 to 800 points. On the other hand, less cooperative groups may end up with joint totals of 550 to 600 points. These results graphically demonstrate to the participants the benefits to be derived from cooperative bargaining. Had the latter negotiators been able to discover the 200 to 250 points they missed, both would have left the table with more generous terms.

---

[99] Even when the only issue to be negotiated concerns the payment of money by one party to another, there may be room for cooperative bargaining. If the parties can agree upon in-kind payments (*e.g.*, the provision of goods or services) or future payments, the receiving party may still obtain what it wants but at less cost to the other side. It thus behooves even money traders to contemplate alternative payment schemes that might prove mutually beneficial.

[100] *See* BIRKE & FOX, *supra* note 42, at 30–31.

[101] *See* MNOOKIN, PEPPET & TULUMELLO, *supra* note 33, at 14–16.

If the Cooperative Stage is to develop successfully, several prerequisites must be established. First, the parties must achieve a tentative accord. Second, at the conclusion of the Closing Stage, one or both parties should suggest movement into the Cooperative Stage. If one side is concerned that the other will be reluctant to progress in this direction until a provisional agreement has been attained, it can suggest that both parties initial the terms they have already agreed upon. Although proficient negotiators may occasionally merge the latter part of the Closing Stage with the introductory portion of the Cooperative Stage, most bargainers only move into the Cooperative Stage after they have reached a mutually acceptable distribution of the pertinent items.[102]

It is crucial that both sides recognize their movement from the Closing to the Cooperative Stage. If one party attempts to move into the Cooperative Stage without the understanding of the other, problems may arise. The alternative proposals articulated may be less advantageous to the other participant than the prior offers. If the recipient of these new positions does not view them as incipient cooperative overtures, she might suspect disingenuous competitive tactics. It is thus imperative that a party contemplating movement toward cooperative bargaining be sure her opponent understands the intended transition. When such a move might not be apparent, this fact should be explicitly communicated.

When the participants enter the Cooperative Stage, they should seek to discover the presence of previously unfound alternatives that might be mutually beneficial. They must work to expand the overall pie to be divided between themselves.[103] They may have failed to consider options that would equally or even more effectively satisfy the underlying needs and interests of one side with less cost to the other party.[104] To accomplish this objective, the participants must be willing to candidly disclose the underlying interests of their respective clients. Although they should have explored many of these factors during the Information, Distributive, and Closing Stages, they may not have done so with complete candor for strategic reasons. Each may have over- or under-stated the value of different items to advance their competitive interests. Once a tentative accord has been achieved, the parties should no longer be afraid of more open discussions.

Both sides must be quite open during the Cooperative Stage if the process is to function effectively. Through the use of objective and relatively neutral inquiries, the participants should explore their respective needs. Negotiators should use brainstorming techniques to develop options not previously considered. They should not be constrained by traditional legal doctrines or conventional business practices, recognizing that they can agree to anything that is lawful. They should not hesitate to think outside the box.[105] When one side asks the other if another resolution would be as good or better for it than what has already been agreed upon, the respondent must be forthright. It is only where the parties have effectively explored all of the possible alternatives that they can truly determine whether their initial agreement optimally satisfies their fundamental needs.

As the participants enter the Cooperative Stage, they must be careful to preserve their credibility. They may have been somewhat deceptive during the Information,

---

[102] *See* DAWSON, *supra* note 13, at 173–74.

[103] *See* MNOOKIN, PEPPET & TULUMELLO, *supra* note 33, at 11–43; FISHER & URY, *supra* note 5, at 58–83.

[104] *See* Karrass, *supra* note 47 at 145.

[105] *See generally* TOM KELLEY, THE ART OF INNOVATION (2001).

Distributive, and Closing Stages with respect to actual client needs and interests. In the Cooperative Stage, they hope to correct the inefficiencies that may have been generated by their prior dissembling. If they are too open regarding their previous misrepresentations, however, their opponents may begin to question the accuracy of all their prior representations and seek to renegotiate the entire accord.[106] This would be a disaster. It is thus imperative that negotiators not overtly undermine their credibility while they seek to improve their respective positions during the Cooperative Stage.

It is important for persons participating in cooperative bargaining to appreciate the competitive undercurrent that is present even during these seemingly win-win discussions. While participants are using cooperative techniques to expand the overall pie and improve the results achieved by both sides, some may also employ competitive tactics to enable them to claim more than their share of the newly discovered areas for mutual gain. For example, if the participants discover an additional "250 points"[107] of client satisfaction that can be divided between themselves, there is nothing that requires them to allocate 125 points to each side. If one party realizes that a proposed modification of the existing agreement could increase her client's situation by 150 or even 200 points, she might disingenuously indicate that the new proposal would be a "slight improvement" to allow her to make her opponent think the new proposal would only expand the overall pie by 75 or 100 points. She would then give her adversary 35 to 50 points, and retain the other 100 to 150 points for her own side.

Once final agreements have been achieved, the parties often hang up the phones or depart for home, thinking that they are finished. As a result, they may fail to ensure a complete meeting of the minds. Before then conclude their interaction, participants should briefly review the specific terms they think have been agreed upon. They may occasionally find misunderstandings. Since they are psychologically committed to agreements, they are likely to resolve their disagreements amicably. If they did not discover the misunderstandings until one side drafted the accord, there might be claims of dishonesty and recriminations. It is thus preferable to confirm the basic terms, before they conclude their encounter.

Most attorneys prefer to draft the terms of agreements achieved, believing that they will do a better job of reflecting their client interests than will their adversaries. They have an ethical duty to include precisely what was agreed upon. On occasions when adversaries draft the settlement agreements, the recipients of such documents should review the terms carefully to be sure they state what was agreed upon. They should look for anything included that was never agreed upon, or the omission of any term which was agreed upon.

---

[106] See Robert Condlin, *Bargaining in the Dark: The Normative Incoherence of Lawyer Dispute Bargaining Role*, 51 MD. L. REV. 1, 44–45 (1992).

[107] In my Legal Negotiation course, I assign point values for each item to be negotiated to apprise students of the relative values placed on the different terms from their respective client perspectives. When representing real clients, attorneys should mentally do the same thing, as they probe underlying client needs and interests. The "essential" terms should have a higher value than the "important" terms, which should be valued more than merely "desirable" issues. While lawyers may not assign exact point values for each item, they should have a good idea of the comparative value of the different terms.

NEGOTIATION EXERCISE

The following exercise should be negotiated, with the participants looking carefully for the transition through the different stages. Participants should form pairs of negotiators, with half being designated the representatives of Plaintiff Jane Doe and half the representatives of Defendant Professor Palsgraf. As you read the General Information and your *own side's* Confidential Information, you should begin the *Preparation Stage*. When you begin your interaction with the other side, you should use the *Preliminary Stage* to establish some rapport with that person and to create a positive negotiating environment. During the *Information Exchange*, you should ask a number of *open-ended* and *"what"* and *"why"* questions to determine the other side's underlying needs and interests, while carefully disclosing your own objectives. Once this *value creation* process is accomplished, you and your opponent should move into the *value claiming Distributive Stage*. Near the end of your interaction, you and your opponent should use the *Closing Stage* to solidify the deal, and finally move into the *Cooperative Stage* to make sure you have both achieved an efficient agreement that maximizes the joint gains achieved by both sides.

GENERAL INFORMATION — SEXUAL HARASSMENT EXERCISE

Last year, Jane Doe was a first year law student at the Yalebridge Law School, which is part of Yalebridge University, a private, non-sectarian institution. Ms. Doe was a student in Professor Alexander Palsgraf's Tort Law class.

During the first semester, Professor Palsgraf made sexually suggestive comments to Ms. Doe on several occasions. These comments were always made outside of the classroom and when no other individuals were present. Ms. Doe unequivocally indicated her personal revulsion toward Professor Palsgraf's remarks and informed him that they were entirely improper and unappreciated.

During the latter part of the second semester, Professor Palsgraf suggested to Ms. Doe in his private office that she have sexual relations with him. Ms. Doe immediately rejected his suggestion and told Professor Palsgraf that he was "a degenerate and disgusting old man who was a disgrace to the teaching profession."

Last June, Ms. Doe received her first year law school grades. She received one "A", two "A-", one "B+", and one "D", the latter grade pertaining to her Tort Law class. She immediately went to see Professor Palsgraf to ask him about her low grade. He said that he was sorry about her "D", but indicated that the result might well have been different had she only acquiesced in his request for sexual favors.

Ms. Doe then had Professor Irving Prosser, who also teaches Tort Law at Yalebridge, review her exam. He said that it was a "most respectable paper" which should certainly have earned her an "A-" or "B+", and possibly even an "A."

Ms. Doe has sued Professor Palsgraf in state court for $250,000 based upon three separate causes of action: (1) sexual harassment in violation of Title IX of the Education Amendments of 1972; (2) intentional infliction of emotional distress; and (3) fraud. Professor Palsgraf has a net worth of $450,000, including the $350,000 equity in his house and a $50,000 library of ancient Gilbert's outlines.

CONFIDENTIAL INFORMATION — JANE DOE

CONFIDENTIAL INFORMATION — JANE DOE

Your client wants to obtain several forms of relief from Professor Palsgraf: (1) a grade of "A" or "A-" in Tort Law; (2) the resignation of Professor Palsgraf from the Yalebridge Law School; and (3) a sufficiently large sum of money to deter such offensive conduct by other professors in the future.

(I) Score *plus 35 points* if Professor Palsgraf agrees to change Ms. Doe's Tort Law grade to "A-", and *plus 50 points* if he agrees to change her grade to "A".

(II) Score *plus 200 points* if Professor Palsgraf agrees to resign from the Yalebridge Law School faculty. If Professor Palsgraf does not resign, but agrees to take a one-year leave of absence *or* a one-year sabbatical leave from the Law School during the *coming* academic year (*i.e.*, Ms. Doe's second year), score *plus 50 points*. If Professor Palsgraf agrees to take a leave of absence and/or sabbatical leave during the coming year *and* the following year (*i.e.*, Ms. Doe's final two years of law school), score *plus 75 points*.

(III) If Professor Palsgraf does not resign, but he does agree to seek psychiatric counseling *and* personally apologize to Ms. Doe, score *plus 50 points*.

(IV) Score *plus 2 points* for *each $1,000*, or part thereof, Professor Palsgraf agrees to immediately pay Ms. Doe in settlement of her suit.

(V) Ms. Doe is concerned about the publicity surrounding this matter and the impact that publicity may have on her future employment opportunities. Score *plus 50 points* for a clause guaranteeing the confidentiality of any settlement reached with Professor Palsgraf.

Since Ms. Doe wishes to have this matter resolved now so that she may concentrate fully on her legal education, you will automatically be placed at the *bottom* of your group if no settlement agreement is achieved.

CONFIDENTIAL INFORMATION — PROFESSOR PALSGRAF

CONFIDENTIAL INFORMATION — PROFESSOR PALSGRAF

Your client realizes that his conduct was entirely inappropriate, and he is deeply sorry for the difficulty he has caused Ms. Doe. He would thus be willing to submit to psychiatric counseling and to personally apologize to Ms. Doe. Should you agree to either or both of these requirements, you lose *no points*.

Professor Palsgraf fears that Ms. Doe may ask for his resignation from the Yalebridge Law School, and he would rather lose everything before he would forfeit his Yalebridge position. Should you agree to have Professor Palsgraf resign his Yalebridge professorship, you must *deduct 500 points*.

Your client recognizes that he will have to provide Ms. Doe with the grade she should have received. He is readily willing to change her grade to "A-", and you lose *no points* for agreeing to an "A-". Professor Palsgraf does not think that Ms. Doe's exam performance was really worthy of an "A". You thus *lose 50 points* if you agree to have Ms. Doe's Tort Law grade changed to an "A".

Professor Palsgraf is currently eligible for a one-year, paid "sabbatical leave." He has been saving this leave to enable him to go to Cambridge University in two years. If you agree to have Professor Palsgraf take that *"sabbatical leave"* during either of the next two academic years, you *lose 25 points*. Should you agree to have him take a *"leave of absence"* during either of the next two academic years, which, unlike a "sabbatical leave," would not involve a continuation of his salary, you *lose 100 points*. (If you agree to both a one-year sabbatical *and* a one-year leave of absence, you *lose* a total of *125 points*.)

Professor Palsgraf will almost certainly have to provide Ms. Doe with monetary compensation for the wrong he committed. You *lose 3 points* for *each $1,000*, or part thereof, you agree to pay Ms. Doe. Any agreement regarding the payment of money must be operative immediately — no form of future compensation may be included.

Professor Palsgraf is concerned about the publicity surrounding this tragic affair. Score *plus 50 points* for a clause guaranteeing the confidentiality of any settlement reached.

Since Professor Palsgraf believes that the continuation of this law suit may ruin his outstanding legal career, you will automatically be placed at the *bottom* of your group if no settlement is achieved.

SELF-ASSESSMENT

SELF-ASSESSMENT

When the exercise is finished, you and your cohorts should use the Exercise Efficiency Grid on the following page to determine how efficiently you all divided the different items. If certain pairs did not maximize their joint returns, they must ask themselves two critical questions. First, did each side tell the other side the different terms they hoped to obtain? Opponents cannot read their minds. If negotiators never indicate what they want, the other side may never appreciate this party's underlying needs and interests. Second, if the other side asked for items this side does not especially value but it has not conceded them and they reach a tentative agreement, this side should ask what it could obtain in return for concessions on those particular terms. For example, if Professor Palsgraf has not agreed to an apology and counseling and/or a sabbatical leave, he should ask Jane Doe what she could do for him if he granted her these terms. She would gain 100 points (+50 for each) and could reduce her monetary total by up to $50,000 (at +2 points per $1000) and be better off. Although Professor Palsgraf would lose 25 points for the sabbatical leave, he would save 3 points for each $1000 Jane Doe reduces her monetary total. Thus, if she were to reduce her monetary total by $30,000 or $40,000, Professor Palsgraf would save minus 90 or minus 120, which would more than offset the 25 points lost for the sabbatical leave.

SEXUAL HARASSMENT EXERCISE EFFICIENCY

A- is **More Efficient** grade than A [Net Gain of 35 pts. for A- vs. 0 pts. for A]

A- generates +35 pts. for Plaintiff at No Cost to Defendant

A generates +50 for Plaintiff, but at cost of -50 to Defendant

If Plaintiff accepts A- and saves Defendant 50 pts., Defendant can afford to give Plaintiff an additional $10,000 to $15,000 — costing Defendant fewer than 50 pts. — while generating extra 20 to 30 pts. for Plaintiff which, when added to +35 for A-, results in more than the +50 Plaintiff would get for A alone.

II.   Personal Apology **and** Psych. Counseling generate +50 for Plaintiff at No Cost to Defendant

By giving Plaintiff +50 here, Plaintiff could reduce Monetary Demand by $25,000 and still gain same +50 — reduction of $25,000 saves Defendant -75 pts. [25 × -3].

III. Resignation generates Net Loss of 300 pts. — Plaintiff gets +200, but Defendant loses 500 pts.

If Defendant willing to lose 500 pts., Plaintiff should seek the $167,000 that would cost Defendant -501 pts. while generating +334 for Plaintiff

IV.   Sabbatical Leave generates Net Gain of 25 pts. — Plus 50 for Plaintiff with only -25 for Defendant

Leave of Absence generates Net Loss of 50 — Plus 50 pts. for Plaintiff, but -100 for Defendant

V.   Confidentiality Clause generates +50 for *each* party. [When first party requests this clause, does opponent immediately agree to it or use it as *false issue* in effort to obtain additional concession for same Confidentiality Clause it also wants?]

VI.   Money is Net Loser — Each $1000 gets +2 pts. for Plaintiff, while costing Defendant -3 pts.

Chapter 4
NEGOTIATION TECHNIQUES

When individuals negotiate, there are a relatively finite number of techniques they can employ to advance their interests. It is beneficial for negotiators to understand the different techniques both to enable them to decide which ones they should use and to allow them to recognize and counteract the tactics being used by their opponents. Although I describe over thirty different techniques in my more expansive legal negotiation text book,[1] I will focus on the most common and interesting ones here.

I. NUMERICALLY SUPERIOR BARGAINING TEAM

Most negotiations are conducted on a one-on-one basis with a single attorney interacting with a single opponent. On some occasions, however, one party may attempt to gain a tactical and psychological advantage by including an extra person or two on their bargaining team. They hope the additional participant(s) will intimidate their lone opponent, and make their multi-person team more capable of discerning the verbal leaks and nonverbal signals being emitted by that person. The extra participant(s) can monitor such signals while their partner is speaking, and provide important feedback when the parties take breaks to determine how the interaction is going.

Individuals who are alone against several opponents should not hesitate to have a partner join the interaction. Even if that person does not speak, she can carefully monitor the verbal messages and nonverbal signals while her co-counsel is actively interacting with the different opponents. Many negotiators prefer to have a more active partner when they interact with opposing teams. That individual may observe an opening they do not see due to their internalizing of the thought process. She can immediately exploit the situation which would be lost if not taken advantage of in a timely manner.

II. EXTREME INITIAL DEMANDS/OFFERS

Some negotiators like to commence bargaining interactions with extreme opening positions. They hope to use this technique to anchor the preliminary discussions. If their adversaries are not thoroughly prepared, they may begin to bargain up or down from these extreme positions instead of ignoring these openings and articulating rational offers or demands of their own. If negotiators hope to enhance the credibility of one-sided opening positions, they should prepare detailed and logical explanations to support their seemingly unreasonable demands or offers. Such an approach creates an aura of legitimacy, and it usually induces opponents to treat such extreme positions more seriously than positions not supported by rational explanations.

People confronted by extreme opening positions should not casually dismiss them, because this approach may lead opponents to believe their wholly one-sided demands or offers are more realistic than they initially thought. Recipients of such offers should politely but firmly indicate that they are completely unreasonable and unworthy of serious discussion. Such communications can induce the original offerors to moderate both their internal objectives and their external position statements in the other side's direction.

---

[1] CHARLES B. CRAVER, EFFECTIVE LEGAL NEGOTIATION AND SETTLEMENT ch. 10 (7th ed. 2012).

III. PROBING QUESTIONS

An effective way to counteract extreme opening positions involves the use of **probing questions**. Offerees can ask offerors a series of questions requiring those persons to explain the rationales supporting each aspect of their opening positions. The questioners should begin with the most finite components where there is little room for significant puffing and then move on to the less finite aspects. If the unreasonable offerors are forced to explain each component, they begin to falter, because it is difficult to defend wholly realistic positions with respect to such finite items as lost wages or the value of real estate. By the time the other side has responded to the different questions propounded, their position is five times what they were initially offering or one-fifth of what they were demanding.

IV. BOULWAREISM — BEST OFFER FIRST BARGAINING

People who dislike the give-and-take of traditional bargaining encounters occasionally seek to short cut the process by beginning with firm and unyielding opening offers. This was the approach taken by Lemuel Boulware, the former labor negotiator for the General Electric Company, who wished to make it clear to workers that they were getting their wage and benefit increases due to corporate generosity rather than union demands. Parties wishing to employ this device must possess a substantial amount of bargaining power, because, if they do not, opponents will simply ignore their offers and do business with someone else. This **take-it-or-leave-it** approach is an affront to opponents who expect to participate meaningfully in the bargaining process and feel they influenced the final terms agreed upon. It is basically a parent-child interaction with the "parent" offerors telling the "child" offerees what they must accept.

The visceral reaction to Boulwareism is to call the offerors' bluff. This may cause a work stoppage or a failed interaction. Some persons deal with this tactic by ignoring the promise of the offerors not to alter their initial positions and by articulating realistic offers of their own. They hope to generate typical adult-to-adult discussions that will allow the initial offerors to begin to retreat from their seemingly resolute positions.

Although Boulwareism may work against less competent negotiators, it will rarely intimidate proficient bargainers. It is likely to turn them off and cause them to contemplate their nonsettlement options. Persons considering the use of best-offer-first tactics should realize the offensive impact such an approach has on opponents. It is more effective for bargainers to begin the discussions with lower offers or higher demands and allow the other side to talk them up or down to where they initially thought the parties would conclude their interactions. This approach is much more likely to satisfy opponents who wish to feel they were respected and allowed to influence the final terms agreed upon. Negotiators tend to be more satisfied with objectively less beneficial results when they feel the bargaining process was fair than with objectively more beneficial results when they feel the process was not fair.[2]

Individuals who employ Boulwareism should recognize two critical risks associated with this tactic. First, its use greatly increases the probability of nonsettlements due to the way it offends take-it-or-leave-it offer recipients. Second, it deprives users of the opportunity to obtain more generous results than those articulated in their

---

[2] *See* Rebecca Hollander-Blumoff, *Just Negotiation*, 88 Wash. U. L. Rev. 381 (2010).

opening positions. Negotiators who begin with lower offers and elevated demands have the chance to test opposing side interests to determine whether they may be able to achieve final terms that are more generous to their own side than they initially thought they could achieve.

V.   LIMITED CLIENT AUTHORITY

Many negotiators like to indicate when they commence bargaining encounters that they lack authority to bind their principals. Some persons who actually possess real authority make such representations to avoid being bound before they have the time to consider terms tentatively agreed upon or to use the Nibble Technique that will be discussed next. Others make such representations based upon the fact they must actually obtain the approval of absent clients before terms can become final.

The advantage of limited authority concerns the ability of such negotiators to bind their opponents without binding themselves. Once their opponents have become psychologically committed to agreements, they are likely to make additional post-"agreement" concessions to preserve the arrangements they think have been achieved.

Negotiators who are told by opponents that such persons lack the authority to bind their principals may wish to indicate a similar constraint on their own side. This means that no agreement can become binding until the principals on *both sides* have had the opportunity to review the tentative terms already reached. Another way to deal with such opponents is to let them know when terms have been preliminarily achieved that this side has absolutely no additional room to move. They can indicate that if the other side demands further changes, the agreement will be lost.

Negotiators who tell opponents that they possess limited authority even when they have a good idea what their clients would accept should never make the mistake of telling someone who has provided them with an unexpectedly generous offer that they will get back to that person in a couple of days after they check with their absent clients. By then, the other side may realize that they have made a mistake and withdraw their offer. The recipients of such an offer should excuse themselves to allow them to contact their client to see if the client would be willing to accept the proffered terms. They can then solidify the deal before the other side can reconsider its offer.

Negotiators should be careful not to interact seriously with opponents who possess *no client authority*. Such persons contact people to find out what they expect to achieve. Once these individuals obtain opening position statements, they indicate that the offers are wholly unacceptable, hoping to induce careless negotiators to bid against themselves with new offers. Negotiators who encounter such adversaries should not succumb to this tactic. They should immediately ask such persons to state their own opening positions. When they indicate a lack of client authority, they should be told to get some authority so they can put their own offer on the table so both sides will be on an equal footing.

VI.   LIMITED TIME OFFERS/DECREASING OFFERS OR INCREASING DEMANDS

During the preliminary stages of some negotiations, a few attorneys make fairly realistic offers or demands they say must be accepted by specific dates. They make it clear that if their offers are not accepted by those dates, they will either withdraw those offers entirely *or* begin to reduce the amounts being offered or increase the amounts being demanded. They hope to employ this tactic to intimidate less proficient opponents to cave in to their positions.

It can be entirely appropriate for negotiators to establish firm dates by which time their offers must be accepted or withdrawn — especially where their principals have other options they may decide to explore. The major risk associated with this tactic concerns the fact their adversaries may not yet be prepared to make binding determinations on such a limited time line. As a result, deals that might have been consummated may be lost.

Over the past several years, I have seen an unusual change in this technique. Persons making opening offers not only set time limits, but also indicate that if their offers are not accepted they will *demand more* or *offer less.* This is an extremely risky approach to bargaining. When other parties begin to move *away from* their starting positions, this will induce most opponents to move toward their nonsettlement alternatives. They either prepare for the trial of litigation matters or look for other business deals

VII. FLINCH/KRUNCH

When negotiators obtain opening offers from opposing parties, they can often generate consecutive opening offers through the use of the **flinch or krunch**.[3] When they receive the opening party's offer, they flinch and look disappointed in that person's excessive demand or parsimonious offer. They hope to induce that individual to bid against himself by way of another position statement. Adept negotiators can also employ this device later in the interaction when they receive bargaining concessions, to induce the person who just changed his position to make consecutive position changes.

Individuals should not permit the flinch of their opponent to induce them to bid against themselves through consecutive opening offers or consecutive concessions. They should ignore such behavior by the other side, and make it clear that they do not plan to alter their current position until they obtain a reciprocal opening offer or position change from that person.

VIII. ANGER/AGGRESSIVE BEHAVIOR

Negotiators occasionally resort to anger or aggressive tactics to convince their opponents of the seriousness of the circumstances involved. They raise their voice, pound the table, and occasionally walk out. They hope to intimidate less confident opponents to give in to their demands. Proficient negotiators almost never lose their tempers, since they recognize that such behavior would be likely to have a negative impact on their interactions. They thus employ this device in a carefully controlled manner. For example, when the Russian Premiere pounded on the table at the United Nations with his shoe, both of his feet still had shoes on them! This was not a spontaneous act, but a planned "tantrum" in which he used a shoe that he had brought into the chamber in his briefcase.

When opponents seem to become angry, most persons respond in kind. This often causes problems as the battle escalates. The best way to respond to strategic "anger" is the opposite of what is expected. If opponents stand over someone and shout, those

---

[3] *See* ROGER DAWSON, SECRETS OF POWER NEGOTIATING 32–35 (3d ed. 2011).

victims should remain calm and silent. They should listen carefully for verbal leaks that may inadvertently disclose important information. They should also look at their opponents as if they are acting like children. It is difficult to have a one-way harangue for long without becoming embarrassed. As the demonstrative parties feel ashamed of their behavior, they tend to make concessions in an effort to regain social acceptability.

IX. WALKING OUT/HANGING UP TELEPHONE

Some especially demonstrative negotiators like to walk out of in-person talks or slam down their telephone receivers. This approach is used to intimidate timid opponents into unplanned concessions. If others walk out or hang up rudely, negotiators should not follow them out the door or call them right back. Such behavior would only embolden them. Such demonstrative bargainers should instead be allowed to leave or to hang up without further interaction. They have to be taught that such tactics will not be rewarded. Once they realize that this approach is not working, they are unlikely to employ it again.

X. IRRATIONAL BEHAVIOR

I am frequently asked what to do when people have to deal with wholly irrational opponents. These individuals behave as if they belong in mental institutions in an effort to intimidate their opponents. It would be extremely rare for professional negotiators to encounter truly irrational opponents, because it is virtually impossible for such persons to survive in the competitive business world. Most persons who appear to be irrational are behaving like foxes. Their conduct is carefully controlled. Adversaries should ignore their strange demeanors and make their planned presentations. When the parties part company, their strangely behaving opponents will evaluate the offers they have received as logically as other negotiators.

A federal district judge once told me that whenever he had a major case scheduled for trial that would take a number of weeks to try, he would ask the attorneys to come to his office for a conference a week or two before the trial date. He would ask them to review the relevant legal issues, which they did very well. When they were finished, he would ask several questions that were completely off the wall. The lawyers would look at each other, walk out, and settle the case. They thought that such a confused judge could not possibly preside over a trial involving such intricate legal issues he seemed incapable of comprehending. He was thus able to keep his calendar clear for other matters.

XI. UPROAR ("CHICKEN LITTLE")

Negotiators occasionally threaten dire consequences if their demands are not met. They hope to convince opponents that they must give in or face total destruction. When someone threatens such extreme consequences, the person being threatened should ask two critical questions. First, it the threatened result likely to result. When they step back and look at the situation objectively, it may become clear that this is an idle threat the other side cannot possibly effectuate. Second, if the threatened consequence may result, how would that situation affect the other side. When someone threatens mutual annihilation, the key word is *"mutual."* Is the other side really willing to destroy itself to get at this side? When they realize that the threat is not having the hoped for impact, they will usually move on to other less drastic techniques.

XII. BRER RABBIT (REVERSE PSYCHOLOGY)

Joel Chandler Harris created the unforgettable character named Brer Rabbit. When he was caught by the fox, he asked to be skinned or to have his eyeballs ripped out, as long as he was not flung in the brier patch. The fox tossed him in the brier patch and he escaped. This technique is based on reverse psychology. People employing this technique indicate a preference for Items 1 and 2, but suggest a willingness to accept Items 3 and 4 if they cannot have what they prefer to obtain. Items 3 and 4 are their real objective. Win-lose opponents will force upon them the items they think they least prefer. They should play the game to the end by suggesting that if this is all they obtain, their client will be disappointed. Their Brer Rabbit adversaries will be relieved to think they have put them in a negative position.

This tactic can be especially effective against highly competitive win-lose opponents who are only satisfied when they think their counterparts have completely lost. They thus try to give others what they think those persons least with to obtain. If the Brer Rabbit approach is used effectively against them, they will force the other side to accept Items 3 and 4 instead of the other two things that side professes to want, causing their counterparts to leave with exactly what they wanted.

XIII. MUTT AND JEFF (GOOD COP/BAD COP)

The Mutt and Jeff routine is one of the most common — and often effective — negotiation tactics. One seemingly reasonable negotiator softens opponent resistance by thanking them for their kind treatment and requesting seemingly modest proposals. Opponents are pleased to give them what they are seeking. As soon as they do, however, the unreasonable partners of these persons completely trash these concessions and demand substantial changes. When the opponents are about to explode, the "good cops" calm their "bad cop" partners and request additional concessions. When they obtain better terms, the bad cops attack the new offers being made. As obvious as this Mutt and Jeff technique can be, it is amazing how often negotiators succumb to these tactics. They work so hard to please the bad cops that they fail to appreciate how effectively they have been fleeced.

Most people confronted with Mutt and Jeff opponents make the mistake of arguing entirely with the bad cops. What they should do is focus on the good cops. When these seemingly reasonable persons indicate they would accept the terms if a couple of modest changes were made, the speakers should be directly asked if they would agree if these modifications were made. The good cops should be forced to say "yes" or "no." Once it becomes clear that they will not say "yes" without the concurrence of their bad cop partners, the game is over and they have to change tactics.

XIV. PASSIVE-AGGRESSIVE BEHAVIOR

These are people who disrupt the bargaining process indirectly. They show up late or fail to bring needed papers to scheduled sessions. They promise to write up agreed upon terms, but fail to do so in a timely manner. They seem disinterested in the interaction, but they are actually very interested parties who are quite aggressive — only they are passively-aggressive. Their aggression is displayed indirectly instead of overtly.

Opponents should take control of the interaction by obtaining the necessary documents and by preparing drafts of particular provisions. They want to preempt the ability of these passive-aggressive individuals to disrupt the bargaining process.

They should work hard to induce these persons to agree to particular terms. Those negotiators will insist upon the right to draft the final agreement. As soon as they leave, these people should draft those terms. When they get together to finalize their previous agreement, the passive-aggressive persons will indicate that they did not have the time to draft the agreed upon terms and even begin to ask for changes. If their opponents present them with a complete draft, they are likely to give up and sign the proffered documents. Once they are faced with a fait accompli, they usually do not have the ability to directly reject what has been placed before them, since such overt action is inconsistent with their passive-aggressive personalities.

XV. BELLY UP

Some sly negotiators emulate the Lt. Columbo character created by Peter Falk and act like bumbling idiots. They say that they don't know anything about these types of interactions and indicate a willingness to allow their "fair and knowledgeable" opponents to determine what would be appropriate for both sides. They hope to lull unsuspecting opponents into careless disclosures and concessions intended to help these seemingly inept bargainers. In the end, these Brer Rabbit negotiators leave with everything, and their opponents are so glad they could help solve their problems. These are highly manipulative negotiators.

Individuals should never feel sorry for seemingly incompetent adversaries. They should ignore such behavior and execute their planned negotiation strategy. They should come out with their planned opening offers/demands. When their opponents act shocked and beg them to reconsider their positions, they should ask those persons to state their own positions. Those manipulative negotiators should be forced to articulate and defend their own positions. It is the last thing they hope to do. They want the other side to make all of the concessions, without them having to meaningfully participate in the concession process. Once the belly-up participants realize that their technique is not working, they will end their charade and interact more normally.

XVI. "NIBBLE" TECHNIQUE

A few negotiators agree to "final" terms with apparent client approval. Their opponents are pleased with the agreements and inform their clients of the good news. Several days later, these bargainers contact their opponents with seeming embarrassment and explain that their clients have to have several "slight changes" before the agreements can become final.[4] Since their unsuspecting opponents are psychologically committed to final agreements and do not wish to allow these modifications to negate their prior efforts, they give in to the requested changes. This allows the nibblers to obtain post-agreement concessions that are not reciprocated by themselves.

The individuals being nibbled usually ask themselves the incorrect question — "are *we* going to let the whole deal fall through over these slight changes?" They need to refocus their attention on the other side and ask: "Are *they* going to let the whole deal fall through over these slight changes?" When they examine the circumstances from the perspective of both sides, they realize that the other side is as interested in a final accord as they are. Those persons are thus not likely to walk away from the deal the

---

[4] *See* DAWSON, *supra* note 3, at 85–92.

parties have already achieved simply because they have been unable to extract post-agreement unilateral concessions from this side.

Individuals confronted by nibbler opponents need to be "*provocable*" if they wish to avoid exploitation. When their opponents inform them of the necessity for modifications, they should demand reciprocity. They should indicate that their clients have some qualms of their own and suggest that they can accommodate the changes being requested if their concerns can be simultaneously satisfied.

If the persons demanding post-agreement changes are actually sincere and their clients really have to have several changes, they will recognize the principle of reciprocity and make concessions in exchange for the modifications they are seeking. If they are disingenuously employing the nibble technique to extract unreciprocated, post-agreement concessions and they are confronted with demands for reciprocity, they will most likely realize that they are better off accepting the original terms agreed upon. They will withdraw their demands for post-agreement modifications.

So long as persons employing the Nibble Technique expressly indicate that they have limited authority and have to obtain client consent before terms can become final, use of the Nibble Technique is considered ethical. On the other hand, if a negotiator indicated that she possessed final authority to bind her side and used this device to obtain one-sided, post-agreement concessions from the other side, this approach would arguably contravene Model Rule 4.1 as a material misrepresentation of fact — whether the negotiator possessed final authority. Persons thinking of using this tactic should thus be careful to indicate that any terms preliminarily agreed upon will still be subject to final client review.

CONCLUSION

When you engage in bargaining interactions, you should be fully aware of the different techniques you are employing, and carefully monitor the reactions of the other side. Do you think your tactics are effectively advancing your interests, or has the opposing side adeptly neutralized them? What techniques are your adversaries employing, and how well have you counteracted them?

Chapter 5
POST-NEGOTIATION ASSESSMENTS

Many attorneys negotiate their way through life without ever trying to learn from their interactions. They simply move from one bargaining encounter to another. They never stop to ask themselves how they are doing and what they could have done differently. If individuals wish to enhance their negotiation proficiency, they should take the time after their more significant interactions to ask themselves how they did. How did the different stages develop? Were they thoroughly prepared? Did they establish good rapport with the other side at the beginning of their interaction and create a positive mood for the discussions? Was there an efficient information exchange? Did they listen carefully for verbal leaks and look for relevant nonverbal signals? How did the distributive and closing stages develop? Did the parties employ the cooperative stage to maximize their joint returns?

What bargaining techniques did they employ, and how did the other side counter them? What tactics did the opposing party employ, and how did they deal with them? Were their initial aspirations too high, appropriate, or too low? Were their opening offers too high, appropriate, or too low? Did they begin with "principled" offers they could logically explain to the other side? Did they encounter any deceitful tactics that went beyond mere puffing or embellishment? Did one side appear to achieve more beneficial results than the other side? If so, how was this accomplished?

What did they *do* during their interaction that they wish they had not done? This question usually focuses upon tactical errors that may have been made. What could they have done differently in this regard? What did they *not do* that they wish they had done? This question usually pertains to something the other side did that they did not know how to handle. If they simply wait until they encounter such a situation in the future, they will probably deal with it then as poorly as they did now. If they really analyze the best way to counter such circumstances and roll play how they will react in future situations, they will be far more likely to handle such circumstances effectively in the future than they did now.

Although it is beneficial for negotiators to ask both what they did that they wish they had not done and what they did not do that they wish they had done, it is important to recognize that the latter question is more likely to enhance their future negotiations than the former inquiry.[1] This difference is due to the fact that individuals who think about what they *did not do* are able to incorporate the missing element(s) in their *future* interactions. On the other hand, persons who think about what they had done that they believe they should hot have done can omit such behavior from their future interactions, but this information will not necessarily induce them to appreciate what they should now do instead.

Readers should use the following Post Negotiation Evaluation Checklist to help them review the negotiation exercises they have already completed. They should also employ it following the other negotiation exercises they work on.

---

[1] *See* Laura Kray, Adam Galinsky & Keith Markman, *Counterfactual Structure and Learning from Experience in Negotiations*, 45 J. EXPERIMENTAL PSYCH. 979 (2009).

POST NEGOTIATION EVALUATION CHECKLIST

1. Was your *pre-negotiation preparation* sufficiently thorough? Were you completely familiar with operative facts and law? Did you fully understand your client's value system?

2. Did you carefully determine your side's *bottom line*? Did you also attempt to estimate the *bottom line* of the *other side*?

3. Was your *initial aspiration level* high enough? Did you have a firm goal for *each issue* to be addressed? If you obtained everything you sought, was this due to fact you did not establish sufficiently high objectives? Was your aspiration level so unrealistic that it provided no meaningful guidance to you?

4. Did you prepare a *principled opening offer* that explained the bases for the positions you were taking?

5. Did your *pre-bargaining prognostications* prove to be accurate? If not, what caused your miscalculations?

6. Which party dictated the *contextual factors* such as time and location? Did these factors influence the negotiations?

7. Did you use the *Preliminary Stage* to establish rapport with your opponent and to create a positive negotiating environment? Did you employ *Attitudinal Bargaining* to modify inappropriate opponent behavior?

8. Did the ***Information Stage*** develop sufficiently to provide participants with the knowledge they needed to understand their respective needs and interests and to enable them to consummate an optimal agreement? Did you ask ***broad, open-ended questions*** to get the other side talking and ***"what" and "why" questions*** to determine what the other side wanted and the interests underlying those positions?

9. Were any unintended ***verbal or nonverbal disclosures*** made? What precipitated such revelations? Were you able to use ***Blocking Techniques*** to prevent the disclosure of sensitive information?

10. Who made the ***first offer***? The first ***"real"*** offer? Was a ***"principled" initial offer*** made by you? By your opponent? How did your ***opponent react*** to ***your initial proposal***? How did ***you react*** to your ***opponent's opening offer***?

11. Were ***consecutive opening offers*** made by one party before the other side disclosed its initial position?

12. What specific ***bargaining techniques*** were employed by your ***opponent*** and how were these tactics countered by you? What else might you have done to counter these tactics?

13. What particular ***negotiation devices*** were employed ***by you*** to advance your position? Did the ***opponent*** appear to ***recognize*** the various negotiating techniques you used, and, if so, how did he/she endeavor to minimize their impact? What ***other tactics*** might you have used to advance your position?

14. Which party made the **first concession** and how was it precipitated? Were **subsequent concessions** made on an alternating basis? You should keep a record of each concession made by you and by your opponent throughout the transaction.

15. Were **"principled" concessions** articulated by you? By your opponent? Did **successive position changes** involve decreasing increments and were those increments relatively reciprocal to the other side's concomitant movement?

16. How did the parties **close the deal** once they realized that they had overlapping needs and interests? Did either side appear to make greater concessions during closing phase?

17. Did the parties resort to **cooperative/integrative bargaining** to maximize their aggregate return?

18. How close to the **mid-point** between the initial **real** offers was the final settlement?

19. How did **time pressures** influence the parties and their respective concession patterns? Try not to ignore the time pressures that affected your opponent.

20. Did either party resort to **deceitful tactics** or deliberate misrepresentations to enhance its situation? Did these pertain to material law or fact, or only to

that side's value system or settlement intentions?

21. What finally induced you *to accept* the terms agreed upon or *to reject* the final offer made by the other party?

22. Did *either party* appear to obtain *more favorable terms* than the other side? If so, how was this result accomplished? What could the *less successful* participant have *done differently* to improve its situation?

23. If *no settlement* was achieved, what might have been done differently with respect to client preparation and/or bargaining developments to produce a different result?

24. What did you do that you *wish* you had *not done*? Do you think your opponent was aware of your mistake? How could you avoid such a mistake in the future?

25. What did you *not do* that you *wish you had done* to advance your own interests or to counteract unexpected opponent behavior? What should you plan to do differently in your future interactions?

Chapter 6
PRE-NEGOTIATION SAME SIDE GROUP EVALUATIONS

As readers explore the negotiation process, it can be beneficial for them to work on at least one negotiation exercise that involves several issues and a relatively wide settlement range. The participants should pair off and decide which persons represent which sides. They should review the General Information sheets and their own side's Confidential Information sheets. After they have all had the opportunity to review everything, one side should leave the room while the other group remains.

A facilitator should ask the members of that group how they evaluate the critical factual and legal issues. Do they think they or their opponents have the stronger bargaining position? What problems do they see with respect to their *own side*? What problems do they think the *other side* will have to confront? Most are likely to overstate their own side's weaknesses and under-estimate those of their opponents. What arguments can they make to support their own side's position? What arguments do they anticipate will be made by the other side?

What do they think should be their opening positions with respect to the more relevant issues? It is amazing how different their viewpoints are likely to be with respect to this question. Some plan to articulate very high demands or low offers, while others contemplate more modest opening position statements. They should be asked how much they really hope to obtain with respect to each of these issues. Some will have substantial aspirations, while others will have modest aspirations.

This group should then be told to leave the room, with the other students being asked to return. The facilitator should go through the identical questions from this side's perspective. When this process is done, the different pairs of students should work on the assigned exercises. When they are done, the facilitator should announce the different results achieved. Despite the group sessions, the results usually vary widely. The individuals who had high aspirations have usually achieved more beneficial results than the persons who had lower aspirations. The facilitator should ask the different participants what their opening positions were. The negotiators are shocked when they discover that several made opening offers that were less beneficial than the results actually obtained by some of the other negotiators on the same side.

This group approach is always interesting, because it allows participants to see how differently others working on the identical exercise perceive the different issues. They are also surprised by the different approaches others plan to take and the different aspiration levels disclosed by their cohorts. They also graphically see how those who expect to obtain more beneficial results usually achieve better terms than those with more modest objectives. They should remember these sessions when they get into practice and are preparing for important bargaining interactions. They may wish to consult with colleagues to see how those individuals would approach the impending negotiations. By obtaining such different perspectives, it should help them to determine how they should plan for their encounters.

Chapter 7
INFLUENCE OF NEGOTIATOR STYLES

I. INTRODUCTION

Attorneys and businesspeople negotiate constantly. Most employ relatively "cooperative" or relatively "competitive" styles.[1] Cooperative bargainers tend to behave more pleasantly, and they strive to generate mutually beneficial agreements. Competitive bargainers are often less pleasant, and they work to obtain optimal results for their own sides. Individuals look forward to interactions with cooperative opponents, but often dread their encounters with competitive adversaries.

Negotiator styles significantly affect bargaining interactions. Which styles are used by more negotiators? Which styles are associated with more proficient negotiators and with less effective bargainers? This chapter will discuss different negotiator styles and the impact of these styles on bargaining encounters.

II. COOPERATIVE/PROBLEM-SOLVING AND COMPETITIVE/ADVERSARIAL STYLES

Most negotiation books divide bargainers into two stylistic groups: (1) Cooperative/Problem-Solvers and (2) Competitive/Adversarials. *Cooperative/Problem-Solving negotiators* are epitomized by the book *Getting to Yes.*[2] These persons move psychologically *toward* their opponents, try to maximize the *joint returns* achieved by the bargaining parties, begin with realistic opening positions, seek reasonable and fair results, behave in a courteous and sincere manner, rely upon objective standards to guide discussions, rarely resort to threats, maximize the disclosure of relevant information, are open and trusting, work diligently to satisfy the underlying interests of themselves and their opponents, are willing to make unilateral concessions, and try to reason with people on the other side.

Competitive/Adversarial negotiators are epitomized by the book *Secrets of Power Negotiating.*[3] These individuals move psychologically *against* their opponents, try to maximize their *own returns*, begin with unrealistic opening offers, seek extreme results, behave in an adversarial and insincere manner, focus primarily on their own positions rather than rely on objective standards, frequently resort to threats, minimize the disclosure of their own information, are closed and untrusting, seek to satisfy the interests of their own side, try to make minimal concessions, and manipulate opponents.[4]

Cooperative/Problem-Solvers readily disclose their critical information, explore the underlying interests of the respective parties, and seek results that maximize the return to both sides. They often explore alternatives that may enable the bargainers to expand the overall pie through tradeoffs that simultaneously advance the interests of both sides. For example, when money is involved, they may agree to future

---

[1] *See* G. Richard Shell, Bargaining for Advantage 9-11 (1999); Donald G. Gifford, Legal Negotiation: Theory and Applications 8-11 (1989); Gerald R. Williams, Legal Negotiation and Settlement 18-39 (1983); Gerald R. Williams & Charles B. Craver Legal Negotiating 12-73 (2007).

[2] Roger R. Fisher & William W. Ury, Getting to Yes (1981).

[3] Roger Dawson, Secrets of Power Negotiating (3d ed. 2011). *See also* Jim Camp, Start with No (2002).

[4] *See* Herbert M. Kritzer, Let's Make a Deal 78–79 (1991).

payments or in-kind payments that satisfy the underlying interests of the respective participants. Competitive/Adversarials engage in disingenuous games-playing. They conceal their negative information, and try to manipulate opponents into giving them deals that maximize the returns for themselves. They may even ignore alternative formulations that might benefit their opponents if those alternatives do not clearly advance their own interests.

In the 1976, Gerald Williams conducted a study among attorneys in Phoenix to determine what percentage of legal negotiators behave in a Cooperative/Problem-Solving and a Competitive/Adversarial manner. He asked respondents to indicate how individuals with whom they had recently interacted conducted their interactions. He found that lawyers considered 65 percent of their colleagues to be Cooperative/Problem-Solvers, 24 percent to be Competitive/Adversarials, and 11 percent to be unclassifiable.[5]

When I ask attorneys who attend my Effective Legal Negotiation programs what percentage of their opponents are Cooperative/Problem-Solvers and Competitive/Adversarials, they usually suggest a fifty-fifty split. They are surprised when I cite Professor Williams' empirical findings. What would account for this discrepancy? *Emotional contagion*: when we interact with others, we are affected by their emotional states. We tend to remember negative experiences more than positive experiences. As a result, if we interact with twenty persons today, fifteen of whom are pleasant Cooperative/Problem-Solvers and five of whom are unpleasant Competitive/Adversarials, we remember the five who were more aggressive and less courteous. We thus over-estimate the number of Competitive/Adversarial opponents we have encountered. When we are given a list containing the names of the twenty people with whom we interacted, we recognize the fact that most were Cooperative/Problem-Solvers.

III. COMPARATIVE EFFECTIVENESS OF COOPERATIVE/PROBLEM-SOLVING AND COMPETITIVE/ADVERSARIAL NEGOTIATORS

When I ask Effective Legal Negotiation course participants to describe the styles of effective negotiators, they usually indicate they are aggressive persons who openly indicate a desire to obtain better results for themselves than they give to their opponents. They often suggest that these advocates may employ discourteous behavior to intimidate weaker opponents. I then ask these respondents what they would do if someone came to their office that afternoon, openly indicated that they were there to clean them out, and exacerbated the circumstances with some gratuitous insults. Would they think that someone has to lose and it might as well be themselves — or would they get up for the interaction to avoid exploitation by such a manipulative adversary? They laugh when they realize how quickly they would change their own demeanor to avoid exploitation. They indicate that they would be hesitant to disclose their critical information, lest their opponents take advantage of their one-sided openness. They also suggest that they would employ more strategic tactics designed to neutralize the competitive behavior of their adversary.

I then ask them how they would react to someone who came to their office, and politely indicated an interest in achieving mutually agreeable terms that would satisfy the underlying interests of both sides. They usually suggest that they would respond

---

[5] *See* WILLIAMS, *supra* note 1, at 19.

in an open and cooperative manner designed to maximize the joint results achieved. By this point, they begin to appreciate how much easier it is to obtain beneficial negotiation results from others when people act in an open and seemingly cooperative fashion. They also recognize how much more difficult it is for openly Competitive/Adversarial bargainers to achieve their one-sided objectives.

Gerald Williams asked the respondents in his study to classify opponents as "effective," "average," and "ineffective" negotiators. They indicated that while 59 percent of Cooperative/Problem-Solvers were "effective" negotiators, only 25 percent of Competitive/ Adversarials were so proficient.[6] On the other hand, while only 3 percent of Cooperative/Problem-Solvers were considered "ineffective" negotiators, 33 percent of Competitive/Adversarials bargainers were placed in that category.

In 1999, Andrea Kupfer Schnedier replicated the Gerald Williams study using attorneys in Milwaukee and Chicago as her data base.[7] Her findings reflect changes that have affected our society in general and the legal profession in particular. People are less pleasant to one another today than they were three decades ago. Many persons have become more impatient and less courteous. "The competitive negotiator described by Williams was not nearly as unpleasant and negative" as the contemporary competitive bargainer.[8]

From a detached perspective, one would expect the less courteous and more repugnant Competitive/Adversarial negotiators described in Professor Schneider's study to be less effective than the less negatively described Competitive/Adversarial bargainers in the Williams study, and this is exactly what Professor Schneider found. While Professor Williams found 25 percent of Competitive/Adversarial negotiators to be "effective," Professor Schneider found only 9 percent of such bargainers to be "effective."[9] This change should be contrasted with the relatively slight decline in the percentage of Cooperative/Problem-Solvers considered to be "effective" negotiators from 59 percent in the Williams study to 54 percent in the Schneider study.[10]

The findings with respect to persons considered "ineffective" negotiators are even starker. Professor Schneider found almost no change in the percentage of Cooperative/Problem-Solvers considered "ineffective" bargainers — an increase from 3 percent to 3.6 percent.[11] She found a profound change, however, with respect to the percentage of Competitive/Adversarials considered to be "ineffective" negotiators, rising from 33 percent in the Williams study to 53 percent in her own study. This increase in perceived ineptitude among Competitive/Adversarial negotiators would most likely be attributable to their more unpleasant demeanors. As they are perceived as more irritating, more stubborn, and more arrogant, opponents would consider them to be less effective bargainers.

In the thirty-five years I have taught Legal Negotiating courses, I have not found proficient Cooperative/Problem-Solvers to be less effective than proficient Competitive/Adversarials. The notion that one must be uncooperative, selfish, manipulative, and even abrasive to be successful is erroneous. To achieve beneficial

---

[6] *See id.*

[7] *See* Andrea Kupfer Schneider, *Shattering Negotiation Myths: Empirical Evidence on the Effectiveness of Negotiation Style*, 7 HARV. NEG. L. REV. 143 (2002).

[8] *See id.* at 187.

[9] *See id.* at 167, 189.

[10] *See id.*

[11] *See id.* at 167.

negotiation results one must only possess the ability to say "no" forcefully and credibly to convince opponents they must enhance their offers if agreements are to be achieved. They can accomplish this objective courteously and quietly, and be as effective as those who do so more demonstrably.

I have only noticed three significant differences with respect to the outcomes achieved by different style negotiators on my course exercises. First, if a truly extreme agreement is reached, the prevailing party is usually a Competitive/Adversarial negotiator. Since Cooperative/Problem-Solving bargainers tend to be more fair-minded, they generally refuse to take unconscionable advantage of inept or weak opponents. Second, Competitive/Adversarial advocates generate more *nonsettlements* than their Cooperative/Problem-Solving cohorts. The extreme positions taken by Competitive/Adversarial bargainers and their frequent use of manipulative and disruptive tactics make it easy for their opponents to accept the consequences associated with nonsettlements.

The third factor concerns the fact that Cooperative/Problem-Solving negotiators usually achieve more efficient combined results than their Competitive/Adversarial colleagues — *i.e.*, they maximize the joint return to the parties. Cooperative/Problem-Solvers are open and trusting individuals who seek to enhance the joint disclosure of information and maximize the overall return to the participants. They are thus more likely to attain higher joint values than more closed and untrusting Competitive/Adversarial bargainers who are primarily interested in the maximization of their own side's results.[12] Advocates who hope to achieve Pareto efficient agreements that benefit both sides must be willing to cooperate sufficiently to permit the participants to explore areas of possible joint gain. While these people may simultaneously seek to maximize their own side's returns, their attempt to enhance opponent interests increases the likelihood of agreement *and* the probability of mutually efficient terms. In addition, the more the participants can expand the pie to be divided between themselves, the more likely each side will obtain more satisfactory results.

IV. INTERACTIONS BETWEEN PERSONS WITH DIFFERENT NEGOTIATING STYLES

When Cooperative/Problem-Solving bargainers interact with other Cooperative/Problem-Solvers, their encounters are usually cooperative. The participants are relatively open with their critical information, and they seek to achieve terms that maximize the joint return of the parties. Interactions between Competitive/Adversarial negotiators are generally competitive, with minimal information disclosure and the use of manipulative tactics to advance each side's own interests.

When Cooperative/Problem-Solvers negotiate with Competitive/Adversarials, their transactions tend to be more competitive than cooperative. If Cooperative/Problem-Solvers are naively open with Competitive/Adversarials who are being less forthcoming, information imbalances develop which favor the more strategic Competitive/Adversarials. As a result, Cooperative/Problem-Solving participants must employ a more competitive approach to avoid the exploitation that would result if they were too open and accommodating with their manipulative and avaricious

---

[12] *See* Robert H. Mnookin & Lee Ross, *Introduction, in* BARRIERS TO CONFLICT RESOLUTION 8–9 (Kenneth Arrow, Robert H. Mnookin, Lee Ross, Amos Tversky & Robert Wilson eds., 1995).

opponents. These cross-style interactions generate less efficient agreements than encounters involving only Cooperative/Problem-Solvers, and they increase the likelihood of nonsettlements.

When Competitive/Adversarial negotiators interact with Cooperative/Problem-Solving bargainers, the Competitive/Adversarial participants may enjoy an advantage if their Cooperative/Problem-Solving opponents behave too cooperatively. Competitive/Adversarials feel more comfortable in openly competitive environments than Cooperative/Problem-Solvers who may feel compelled to behave in an uncharacteristically competitive fashion to avoid exploitation. Competitive/Adversarials tend to have higher client goals than Cooperative/Problem-Solving adversaries, and they are less concerned about the joint returns achieved. Less strategic Cooperative/Problem-Solvers are likely to disclose more of their critical information than their less forthcoming adversaries, providing the Competitive/Adversarial bargainers with an information-imbalance advantage.

When Cooperative/Problem-Solvers begin their interactions with persons they do not know well, they should release some confidential information slowly. If their openness is reciprocated, they can continue their openness. On the other hand, if they realize that their openness is not being reciprocated, they should be less forthcoming to avoid the creation of an information imbalance that would be injurious to their own interests.

V.   THE COMPETITIVE/PROBLEM-SOLVING APPROACH

In his study, Professor Williams found that certain traits are shared by both effective Cooperative/Problem-Solving negotiators and effective Competitive/Adversarial bargainers. Successful negotiators from both groups are thoroughly prepared, behave in an honest and ethical manner, are perceptive readers of others, and are analytical, realistic, and convincing.[13] He also found that proficient negotiators from both groups endeavor to *maximize* their **own client's return**. This was the Number One objective for Competitive/Adversarial bargainers and the Number Two objective for Cooperative/Problem-Solving bargainers. In her more recent study, Professor Schneider also found that effective Cooperative/ Problem-Solving negotiators *and* effective Competitive/Adversarial bargainers strive to maximize their own client results.[14] Since client maximization is the quintessential characteristic of Competitive/Adversarial negotiators, this common trait would suggest that many effective negotiators who are identified by their peers as Cooperative/Problem-Solvers are really wolves in sheepskin. These *Competitive/ Problem-Solving negotiators* exude a cooperative style, but seek competitive objectives.

Most successful negotiators are able to combine the most salient traits associated with the Cooperative/Problem-Solving *and* the Competitive/Adversarial styles.[15] They seek to maximize client returns, but attempt to accomplish this objective in a congenial and seemingly ingenuous manner.[16] Unlike less proficient negotiators who

---

[13] *See* WILLIAMS, *supra* note 1, at 20-30.

[14] *See* Schneider, *supra* note 7, at 188. This was again the Number One goal for Cooperative/Problem-Solvers and the Number Two goal for Competitive/Adversarials.

[15] *See* JAMES C. FREUND, SMART NEGOTIATING 24–27 (1992); KRITZER, *supra* note 4, at 78–79; BOB WOOLF, FRIENDLY PERSUASION 34–35 (1990).

[16] *See* ROBERT MAYER, POWER PLAYS 7–8, 92 (1996).

view bargaining encounters as "fixed pie" endeavors in which one side's gain is the other side's corresponding loss, effective Competitive/ Problem-Solving bargainers realize that in multi-item interactions the parties generally value the various terms differently.[17]

They attempt to claim more of the distributive items desired by both sides,[18] but they simultaneously look for shared values. They recognize that by maximizing the joint returns, they are more likely to maximize the settlements achieved for their own clients. These Competitive/ Problem-Solvers seek what Ronald Shapiro and Mark Jankowski characterize as WIN-win results — optimal deals for themselves while providing opponents with the best terms possible given what they have achieved for themselves.[19]

Proficient Competitive/Problem-Solving and Competitive/Adversarial negotiators may manipulate opponent perceptions to enable them to achieve their own goals, but they rarely resort to truly deceitful tactics. They engage in "puffing" and "embellishment," but never misrepresent material information.[20] The realize that a loss of credibility would undermine their ability to achieve beneficial results for themselves. If opponents cannot believe their representations, it would be extremely difficult to induce adversaries to disclose their true underlying interests in ways that would enable the parties to expand the pie and maximize their joint returns.

Despite the fact that effective Competitive/Problem-Solving bargainers generally hope to attain as much as they can for themselves, they are not "win-lose" negotiators. They never judge their own success by asking how poorly their opponents have done. They recognize that the imposition of bad terms on their adversaries does not necessarily benefit themselves. All other factors being equal, they hope to maximize opponent satisfaction as long as this does not necessitate significant concessions on their own part. When they conclude bargaining interactions, they do not compare their own results with the terms achieved by their opponents. They instead ask whether they like what they got, realizing that if they attained their objectives they had successful encounters.

Proficient Competitive/Problem-Solving negotiators do not necessarily seek to maximize opponent returns for purely altruistic reasons. They understand that this approach will most effectively allow them to advance their own interests. First, they have to provide adversaries with sufficiently generous terms to induce them to accept agreements. Second, they want to be sure opponents will honor the deals agreed upon. If they experience post-agreement "buyers remorse," they may try to get out of the deal. Finally, they acknowledge the likelihood they will encounter their adversaries in the future. If those persons remember them pleasantly as courteous and professional negotiators, their future bargaining interactions are likely to be successful.

Effective Competitive/Problem-Solvers and effective Competitive/Adversarials realize that people tend to work most diligently to satisfy the needs of opponents they

---

[17] *See* Robert H. Mnookin, Scott R. Peppet & Andrew S. Tulumello, Beyond Winning 14–15, 174 (2000).

[18] *See* Gary S. Goodpaster, *A Primer on Competitive Bargaining*, 1996 J. Disp. Res. 325 (1996); Gerald B. Wetlaufer, *The Limits of Integrative Bargaining*, 85 Geo. L. Rev. 369 (1996).

[19] *See* Ronald M. Shapiro & Mark A. Jankowski, The Power of Nice 45-61 (2001).

[20] *See generally* Charles B. Craver, *Negotiation Ethics: How to Be Deceptive Without Being Dishonest/ How to Be Assertive Without Being Offensive*, 38 S. Tex. L. Rev. 713 (1997).

like personally.[21] Overtly Competitive/Adversarial bargainers are rarely perceived as likeable. They exude competition and manipulation, and they generate similar responses from opponents. Seemingly cooperative negotiators, however, appear to seek results that benefit both sides. Since others enjoy interacting with them, these individuals find it easier to induce unsuspecting opponents to lower their guard, behave more cooperatively, and make greater concessions.[22]

Competitive/Problem-Solving negotiators really employ a composite style. They seek competitive objectives (maximum client returns), but endeavor to accomplish their goals through problem-solving strategies. This phenomenon may partially explain why Professors Williams and Schneider found more effective Cooperative/Problem-Solving negotiators than effective Competitive/Adversarial bargainers. It is likely that many effective Competitive/Problem-Solving negotiators were so successful in their use of "problem-solving" tactics, that they induced opponents to characterize them as Cooperative/Problem-Solvers rather than as Competitive/Problem-Solvers — or as Competitive/Adversarials in the dichotomous system being employed in the Williams and Schneider studies.

Over the past several decades, legal practitioners have become less polite toward one another. Many have become more win-lose oriented. They seem to fear that if their opponents get what they want, they will be unable to achieve their own goals. These changing attitudes are adversely affecting legal practice in general and bargaining interactions in particular. Experienced attorneys who participate in my Effective Legal Negotiation programs regularly bemoan the decreasing civility they encounter in daily practice. Lawyers who encounter rudeness from opposing counsel should recognize that such inappropriate behavior is *not* a sign of negotiator proficiency, but just the opposite. Uncivilized behavior is a substitute for bargaining competence. Skilled negotiators do not engage in offensive conduct. They recognize that such behavior is unlikely to induce adversaries to give them what they desire. When we like opponents, we want to satisfy their needs and hate to say "no" to them; when we dislike opponents, we actually look for ways to deny them what they want.

Another critical reason for behaving professionally during bargaining encounters concerns recent studies indicating that people who commence negotiations in positive moods bargain more cooperatively, while individuals who begin in negative moods bargain more adversarially.[23] As a result, negotiator pairs who begin bargaining interactions with positive moods achieve larger joint gains than negotiator pairs who begin with negative moods. Persons who behave badly when they negotiate are likely to generate negative moods in their opponents, thus increasing the probability of avoidable nonsettlements. They also decrease the likelihood of Pareto efficient agreements when deals are achieved.

Legal practitioners should not take the negotiation process personally. They must recognize that their opponents have nothing against them personally — those persons are merely endeavoring to advance the interests of their own clients. Attorneys should never view adversaries as the "enemy." Those individuals are actually their

---

[21] *See* ROY J. LEWICKI, JOSEPH A. LITTERER, JOHN W. MINTON & DAVID M. SAUNDERS, NEGOTIATION 219–220 (1994).

[22] *See* GIFFORD, *supra* note 1, at 15–16.

[23] *See* Clark Freshman, Adele Hayes & Greg Feldman, *The Lawyer-Negotiator as Mood Scientist: What We Know and Don't Know About How Mood Relates to Successful Negotiation*, 2002 J. DISP. RES. 13, 15, 19, 22–23; Joseph P. Forgas, *On Feeling Good and Getting Your Way: Mood Effects on Negotiator Cognition and Bargaining Strategies*, 74 J. PERSONALITY & SOC. PSYCH. 565, 566–68 (1998).

best friends, because they are enabling the lawyers with whom they are interacting to earn a living. If no one was at the other end of the telephone line or sitting across the bargaining table from them, they would be unemployed. There would be no business arrangements to structure, no licensing agreements to develop, and no disputes to resolve.

VI.   CONCLUSION

Most experts classify negotiators as Cooperative/Problem-Solvers or Competitive/Adversarials. The former work to achieve reasonable agreements that satisfy the underlying interests of both sides and maximize the joint returns attained, while the latter seek more one-sided arrangements favoring their own sides. More Cooperative/Problem-Solvers are considered effective negotiators than Competitive/Adversarials, and far more Competitive/Adversarials are perceived as ineffective bargainers than Cooperative/Problem-Solvers. The most effective negotiators employ a hybrid Competitive/Problem-Solving style which incorporates the optimal traits from both classifications. They competitively seek to maximize their own returns, but simultaneously seek to expand the overall pie and maximize opponent returns once they achieve their own objectives. These negotiators recognize that they are more likely to achieve their own goals if they exude a cooperative attitude and behave professionally. They also realize that their use of courteous conduct is more likely to generate positive moods in bargaining participants that increase the probability of cooperative behavior and the maximization of joint returns. They never take the process personally, acknowledging that their opponents are merely advocates for the opposing sides who are enabling them to earn a living.

PRISONER'S DILEMMA EXERCISE

The Prisoner's Dilemma Exercise provides a wonderful opportunity to demonstrate the benefits and risks of a cooperative approach. As individuals decide whether to cooperate or defect, they must imagine what their opponent will do and try to minimize the risk they are exposing themselves to exploitation by a manipulative adversary.

Assume that you and your partner have been arrested for a crime that you committed together. The prosecution wants at least one of you to confess to ensure the conviction of both. If only one confesses, he/she will be treated leniently, while the silent partner will be severely punished. If neither confesses, both will receive relatively short prison terms. If both confess, more substantial terms will be given to both. The problem is represented by the following diagram:

	PRISONER B	
	Does Not Confess	Does Confess
Does Not Confess	2 Years for A	10 Years for A
	2 Years for B*	6 Months for B
PRISONER A		
Does Confess	6 Months for A	5 Years for A
	10 Years for B	5 Years for B**

* Cooperative Solution — Best combined result for *both*.

** Minimax Solution — Solution that offers *each* the greatest promise of success in view of opponent's alternative capabilities.

PARTICIPANT INSTRUCTIONS

The readers and their colleagues should pair off. They should then do five iterations of the Prisoner's Dilemma Exercise. For each iteration, each person must write down "yes" or "no" — with "yes" indicating that the person has confessed and with "no" indicating that the person has not confessed. After the first iteration, the two participants display their respective responses and determine the sentence each would receive. They then go on to the second, third, fourth, and fifth iterations, displaying their answers simultaneously *after each* and calculating their respective jail terms. When they are done, they should determine the total number of years each would have to serve from the five iterations combined.

If the participants have cooperated, both would have said "no" for each iteration, resulting in total jail terms of ten years for each (2 yrs. for each iteration). They should then ask how many have had to serve longer total terms, and a number usually have to do so. They should next consider how many pairs cooperated during the first four iterations, only to have one participant "defect" with a "yes" response during the fifth iteration. Several pairs usually reveal such an approach. Other pairs have longer jail terms, because one decided to defect with a "yes" response early, and they both resorted to "yes" responses in subsequent iterations to avoid exploitation.

The participants should do five more iterations, with the rules slightly changed. Each should verbally indicate to the other how they plan to respond at the beginning of each iteration, then they must write down what they actually plan to do. They are not obliged to write down the response they verbally said they would use. *After each iteration*, they simultaneously display their written responses and calculate their respective jail terms. They then go on to the second, third, fourth, and fifth iterations using the identical approach — verbal statements followed by written responses, with the written responses controlling their actual outcomes. They should calculate their total jail terms based upon the five iterations. When they consider how many pairs each achieved ten year totals, more have usually done so than after the first five iterations when they could not verbally communicate their intentions prior to their written responses. It is still likely that several participants defected with "yes" responses on the fifth iteration, and a few defected earlier and generated more joint "yes" responses resulting in longer jail terms for both participants. What this second series demonstrates is the fact that when participants can first indicate what they supposedly plan to do, more actually respond in writing the way they said they would as if they felt a moral obligation to do so.

When my classes have completed the Prisoner's Dilemma Exercise, I talk about the study described in Robert Axelrod's book *The Evolution of Cooperation* (1984). He conducted a computer-based Prisoner's Dilemma competition that was won by Anatol Rapoport's *"Tit-for-Tat"* approach. His system began with a cooperative "no" response, then did on each successive iteration exactly what the other side's program had done on the preceding iteration. Although his program never beat the other side, it generated such jointly beneficial results that over the entire competition his program achieved the best overall results.

Although competitive tendencies are inherently associated with legal negotiations, attorneys can minimize adversarial behavior by following Anatol Rapoport's rules designed to encourage cooperative rather than competitive interactions.

1. ***Do Not Be Envious of Other Side's Success*** — Base your evaluation of transaction on the value to your own side and not on how well you think you have done vis-a-vis your opponent (*i.e.* don't be "win-lose" negotiator).

2. ***Do Not Be First Party to Employ Inappropriate Tactics*** — Begin with cooperative approach designed to encourage reciprocal behavior.

3. ***Be Provocable*** — Be prepared to punish defection by opponent with your own comparable defection to deter future transgressions.

4. ***Be Forgiving*** — When opponent resumes cooperative behavior, you should do likewise and indicate future interest in cooperative behavior.

5. ***Be Transparent and Establish Appropriate Reputation*** — Act in a sufficiently consistent manner that opponents understand your willingness to cooperate — and to retaliate when necessary to deter inappropriate conduct.

COOPERATIVE/PROBLEM-SOLVING — COMPETITIVE/ADVERSARIAL NEGOTIATION EXERCISE

Readers should pair off and work on a multiple item negotiation exercise with the usual General Information and Confidential Information. Half of the individuals on Side A should behave in a Cooperative/Problem-Solving manner. They should be open with their critical information, and begin with realistic opening offers. They should try to generate results that are fair to both sides. The other half of the persons on Side A should behave in a Competitive/Adversarial manner. They should limit their disclosure of critical information, and begin with more extreme opening offers. They may over- and under-state the value of the items being exchanged for strategic purposes. They should try to generate results that maximize their own side's results.

The participants on Side B should also divide into two groups, with one group behaving in a Coperative/Problem-Solving manner and the other in a Competitive/Adversarial way. Individuals on Side A who will employ the Cooperative/ Problem-Solving style should be paired with persons on Side B who will use the Competitive/Adversarial style, and vice versa. They should then work to achieve agreements using the approaches they agreed to follow.

The following Largecorp-Singlepart Exercise can be effectively employed to test the impact of negotiator styles on bargaining interactions.

SINGLEPART-LARGECORP PURCHASE AGREEMENT
GENERAL INFORMATION

Fifteen years ago, Singlepart, Inc., a stereo speaker component manufacturer, was started in a garage. Today, Singlepart, a privately held company, has 50 employees, including 8 electrical engineers, and 32 well-paid assembly line workers. Singlepart owns numerous patents, and has an outstanding reputation. HIGH TECH. NEWS has praised Singlepart "for being on the cutting edge of technology, continually innovating and improving its products, and having a unique approach to component manufacture." While many companies make similar components, Singlepart components are considered the best available.

Six months ago, Largecorp initiated efforts to acquire Singlepart. Preliminary negotiations have been completed. A purchase concept outlining the selling price, the items to be transferred, and other basic terms has been orally agreed to by both parties. Largecorp attorneys were instructed to draft a formal Agreement for Sale of the business.

A Largecorp attorney wrote the attached Agreement for Sale of the business and sent it to Bill Stewart, the President and Owner of Singlepart, and to the Chairman and CEO of Largecorp for their approval. Stewart and the CEO of Largecorp have instructed their attorneys to meet one last time to finalize the precise terms and sign the agreement. As soon as the final terms are agreed upon and the closing date is specified, the Agreement for Sale will become binding.

AGREEMENT FOR SALE OF BUSINESS

This agreement is between *Largecorp*, Buyer, and *William Stewart*, Seller.

RECITALS

A.   Seller is the owner of certain real property, including land, buildings, and improvements, located at 110 Main Street, Neeto City, West Dakota, referred to as "the property."

B.   Seller is the owner and operator of Singlepart, Inc., a stereo speaker component manufacturer, operated on the property ("the business").

C.   Buyer and Seller desire to enter into this agreement for the purchase and sale of the property and the business.

D.   Therefore, the parties agree as follows:

SECTION ONE — OFFER

Buyer agrees to buy from Seller and Seller agrees to sell to Buyer the property and the business, subject to the conditions set forth herein.

SECTION TWO — DESCRIPTION OF PROPERTY AND BUSINESS

The legal description of the real estate included in the property is set forth on page 147 of Book 173 of the Record of Deeds, which is incorporated by reference. The property also includes Singlepart, Inc., the building, equipment, furniture, fixtures, and other improvements located on the described land. The business includes all customer lists, telephone listings, licenses and permits, business and professional memberships, the trade name, patent rights, and all other tangible and intangible property, used in or related to the operation of Singlepart, Inc.

SECTION THREE — PURCHASE PRICE AND TERMS

The purchase price for the property, business, inventory and supplies is $_____.

SECTION FOUR — NON-COMPETITION OBLIGATION

Seller agrees that neither Seller nor any entity in which Seller has an interest as owner, officer, or manager, will open, operate, or in any way become involved in any stereo component research, development, manufacture, or sales business for a period of 5 years after the closing.

SECTION FIVE — WARRANTY AND INDEMNIFICATION PROVISIONS

[To be agreed upon during final negotiations between parties]

SECTION SIX — CLOSING MATTERS

Buyer and Seller will close this sale on or before _____ (date) subject to the satisfaction of all conditions set forth in this agreement. Seller will transfer possession of and title to the property and the business to Buyer at the closing.

SECTION SEVEN — SIGNATURES

_____   _____

      Buyer   Seller

CONFIDENTIAL INFORMATION FOR SINGLEPART ATTORNEYS

CONFIDENTIAL INFORMATION FOR SINGLEPART ATTORNEYS

1. Stewart, the President and sole stockholder, has thought about selling Singlepart for many years but resisted because it was his own creation. Largecorp's offer is rather generous, and Stewart has decided to sell his assets, take time off, and travel. Stewart is proud of his accomplishment with Singlepart. The company weathered the 2000 economic downturn without layoffs, and few workers have left voluntarily — the employees are loyal and deeply committed to their work. Stewart set up specialized management, engineering, and manufacturing work groups, and is convinced that this structure has been the key to Singlepart's success. His greatest concern is that a sale may result in layoffs or splitting up of the long-standing work groups.

2. Several Singlepart employees were interviewed by Largecorp. They were asked numerous questions regarding the effectiveness of the work groups and how they felt about working in new groups. Steward suspects that Largecorp intends to break up Singlepart by changing the management and engineering groups and laying off administrative staff. There is a rumor that six Largecorp engineers would work on projects presently staffed by Singlepart. This is a new development that Stewart wants you to raise today. He is infuriated and may call off the deal — unless he is assured that his work over the past 15 years will not be dismantled by Largecorp. Stewart has also hinted that if the work groups are eliminated and component quality suffers, he may decide to go back into the stereo speaker business.

3. Largecorp is Singlepart's primary customer, and Stewart is concerned that if negotiations are unsuccessful, Singlepart will lose Largecorp's business. As a result, if you fail to reach a final purchase-sales agreement with Largecorp, you will have failed Stewart and be placed at the **bottom** of Singlepart groups.

4. The following is an up-to-date outline of the terms that have been tentatively agreed upon. Stewart realizes that negotiations regarding job protections for his employees may require some changes in the agreement. He has instructed you to finalize the deal as quickly as possible.

EMPLOYEES (the most important issue):

The first choice is to include a clause in the sale agreement guaranteeing each employee (including administrative staff) a minimum **5-year** employment contract **and** maintaining the existing work group structure. If you obtain **both** of these guarantees, score **plus 100 pts.**

The second choice is a clause guaranteeing each employee a minimum 5-year employment contract, but permitting changes in the existing work group structure. If you obtain this promise, score **plus 50 pts.**

For an employment guarantee of **4 years plus 40**; of **3 years plus 30**; and of **2 years plus 20** (regardless of whether the existing work group structure is to be maintained).

Anything with **less** than a **2-year** employment contract guarantee is unacceptable, no matter what concessions Largecorp offers with respect to the maintenance of the existing work group structure. For any employment guarantee of **less than 2 years, minus 50 pts.**

PRICE (the second most important concern):

$10,000,000 was Stewart's initial asking price, and he would still like to get more than the $7,500,000 that is presently being offered by Largecorp. Score **plus 1 pt.** for **each $20,000**, or part thereof, you obtain **over $7,500,000**.

Anything less than $7,500,000 is unacceptable. Score **minus 5 pts.** for **each $10,000**, or part thereof, agreed to **below $7,500,000**.

NON-COMPETITION (the third most important concern):

Although Stewart would prefer to avoid any non-competition obligation, he would be willing to bind himself to a term of no more than 3 years duration, since he would not be likely to return to the stereo component business during that period.

If you eliminate the non-competition obligation entirely, score *plus 25 pts.* If you agree to a non-competition clause of *no more* than *3 years*, score *plus 15 pts.* If you agree to a non-competition clause of *over 3 years*, score *minus 10 pts.* for *each year*, or part thereof, agreed to *in excess* of 3 years.

WARRANTY AND INDEMNIFICATION PROVISIONS

Singlepart believes that Largecorp will request a Warranty Clause stating that Singlepart warrants that there are *no known* environmental problems. Since Singlepart officers are aware of no such problems, you *lose no points* for such a warranty. On the other hand, if you agree to a warranty provision stating that there are *no known or unknown* environmental problems, score *minus 75 points*.

Largecorp may also request an Indemnification Provision obliging Singlepart to indemnify it for any environmental problems discovered on the former Singlepart premises in the coming years. Score *minus 30 points* for an Environmental Indemnification Provision of *up to 2 years* in duration and *minus 100 points* for any Environmental Indemnification Provision *exceeding 2 years* in duration.

Largecorp may request a Liquidated Damage Provision that would apply to its discovery — prior to the closing date — of any financial misrepresentations by Singlepart agents. Since you believe that all financial representations have been accurate, score *minus 10 points* for any liquidated damage clause — of *up to $150,000* — pertaining to financial misrepresentations by Singlepart agents. For a liquidated damage clause *exceeding $150,000*, you must score *minus 50 points*.

5. Do not forget to discuss the *closing date*. Stewart is in no hurry to turn over the company, so if Largecorp wants to wait three or four months, that's fine with him — the South Pacific is warm and sunny all year long. Stewart would like some time to prepare his employees for the change. Score *plus 5 pts.* for *each month*, or part thereof, you post postpone the closing date — up to a maximum or 6 months.

CONFIDENTIAL INFORMATION FOR LARGECORP ATTORNEYS

CONFIDENTIAL INFORMATION FOR LARGECORP ATTORNEYS

1. Largecorp hopes that this acquisition will (1) reduce its costs by enabling it to produce the components it is currently purchasing from Singlepart and (2) improve firm efficiency and creativity by inculcating Singlepart's corporate philosophy throughout Largecorp. Largecorp has interviewed members of various Singlepart work groups to gather information about how Singlepart works and why it has been so successful. The interviewers detected some hostility towards change and concern about future employment security, and you are surprised that employment contracts and office organization have not been part of the negotiations. You hope these issues won't be raised today. Largecorp would like to select a closing date, shake hands, and sign the contract as quickly as possible.

2. If some unexpected issues arise, you must remain pleasant because if negotiations turn bitter and the deal falls apart, Singlepart may refuse to sell to you in the future. Should you fail to achieve a final sales-purchase agreement, you will have failed Largecorp and be placed at the ***bottom*** of Largecorp negotiating groups.

3. Largecorp's CEO likes the agreement as it stands. If concessions need to be made, he wants to compromise as little as possible. The following issues are the most important to him.

PRICE (most important issue):

Largecorp initially offered $7,500,000, but this was not accepted. After interviewing some of Singlepart's employees, you realized that Singlepart is worth much more — up to $10,000,000. You are thus willing to go somewhat above the original $7,500,000 figure if necessary to close the deal. For ***each $20,000***, or part thereof, ***over $8,500,000*** — up to $10,000,000 — agreed to, score ***minus 1 pt.*** In addition, for ***each $10,000***, or part thereof, ***over $10,000,000***, score ***minus 5 pts.***

NON-COMPETITION (second most important issue):

Since Largecorp is purchasing Singlepart to reduce the cost of high-quality components, it would like as little future competition from Stewart as possible. Largecorp fears that Stewart will soon be bored and reenter the stereo component business as a competitor (perhaps even rehiring his former engineers). Largecorp is willing to pay a premium to keep Stewart out of the market. A Largecorp attorney informed you that long-term non-competition clauses are frowned upon by the courts of this state. She told you that a court would almost certainly strike down any non-competition clause in excess of 5 years.

Largecorp and Stewart have tentatively agreed to a five-year term. In five years, start-up costs will have skyrocketed and technology will have advanced so that new companies would have a difficult time breaking into the market. If a shorter period were specified, there would be a risk that Stewart would begin a new venture.

If you obtain a non-competition clause of ***5 years*** in length, score ***plus 75 pts.*** If you agree to a non-competition clause of ***at least 2 years*** but ***less than 5 years***, score ***plus 20 points — plus an additional 10 points*** for ***each year***, or part thereof, ***over 2 years***. If you fail to obtain a non-competition clause of ***at least 2 years***, you ***lose 25 points***.

EMPLOYEES (third most important issue):

Largecorp is still not sure how best to use Singlepart's employees. It has explored various options such as breaking up Singlepart and reassigning its employees and resources throughout the existing Largecorp structure, leaving Singlepart as an independent entity (a wholly-owned subsidiary), and different "in-between" ideas that would maintain some of Singlepart's existing work groups and break up others.

Largecorp executives want to acquire Singlepart first and then try different options to determine which one works best. They like the fact the contract does not specify which Singlepart employees will be retained and for how long and how Singlepart's work groups should be structured. If Singlepart tries to obtain more precise agreements on these issues, you should try to maintain as much flexibility for Largecorp as possible.

Should you agree to any future employment guarantees or work group maintenance obligations, you will be scored as follows:

If you include *no* continuing *employment guarantees* for former Singlepart employees, *plus 40 pts.*

If you guarantee Singlepart employees employment for no more than 3 years, *0 pts.*

For any employment guarantee *in excess* of *3 years*, *minus 10 pts.* for *each year*, or part thereof, *over 3 years*.

Largecorp would like to retain discretion concerning future *work group configurations*. If you restrict Largecorp's discretion with respect to future work group configurations, *minus 20 pts.*

WARRANTY AND INDEMNIFICATION PROVISIONS

Largecorp is always concerned about possible environmental problems discovered after it has purchased other companies. Score *plus 25 pts.* for a Warranty Provision from Singlepart stating that there are *no known* environmental problems. Score *plus 50 pts.* for a Warranty Provision stating that there are *no known or unknown* environmental problems.

Largecorp would like to obtain an Indemnification Provision obliging Singlepart to indemnify Largecorp for any environmental problems discovered on the former Singlepart premises in the coming years. Score *plus 50 pts.* for an Environmental Indemnification Provision of *2 years duration*. Score *plus 75 pts.* for an Environmental Indemnification Provision of *5 years duration*.

Largecorp would like to obtain a Liquidated Damage Provision that would require Singlepart to give it $100,000 in case it discovers — prior to the closing date — any financial misrepresentations by Singlepart agents. Score *plus 30 pts.* for such a Liquidated Damage Provision.

4. Don't forget to decide on the *closing date*. Largecorp would like to close the deal quickly, but recognizes that it may take several months for Stewart to finalize everything. You thus lose *no points* for an agreement to postpone the closing for *up to three months*. Score *minus 8 pts.* for *each month*, or part thereof, you postpone the final closing date *past the third month* — up to *6 months from now*. For *each month*, or part thereof, *beyond 6 months*, score *minus 25 pts.*

SELF-ASSESSMENT

SELF-ASSESSMENT

The Efficiency Point Grid on the following page can be used to demonstrate how certain items should have been resolved to generate the most efficient agreements. Even though Singlepart was willing to accept as little as $7.5 million, Largecorp should have been willing to pay at least $8.5 million. Why would it pay more than it had to pay? To get more "points" for its own side. By giving Singlepart $8.5 million, this generates 50 points for Singlepart at no cost to Largecorp. This enables Singlepart to agree to a five-year Non-Compete Clause which costs it 20 points — 30 points less than the 50 points it obtained from the extra million dollars — and it provides Largecorp with a total of 75 points [+20 for the general Non-Compete Clause +10 points for each year over 2]. The parties should make similarly efficient exchanges with respect to the Employee Guarantees, the Warranty and Indemnification Provisions, and the Closing Date.

When the exercise is over, the different results should be compared to see whether the Competitive/Adversarial participants achieved better results from their own side's perspective than their Cooperative/Problem-Solving opponents. If one group of negotiators behave in a Competitive/ Adversarial manner while their opponents behave in a Cooperative/Problem-Solving manner, the Competitive/Adversarial nego-tiators usually achieve more advantageous results for their own sides. On the other hand, if the persons assigned the Cooperative/Problem-Solving approach had been allowed to modify their behavior to be more strategic to counteract the Competitive/ Adversarial tactics of their opponents, the Cooperative/Problem-Solver participants are no longer at a disadvantage.

Did the tactics of the Competitive/Adversarial participants decrease the likelihood of Pareto superior agreements by preventing the negotiators from being sufficiently candid with respect to their real objectives? If the Competitive/Adversarial bargainers had employed the more moderate Competitive/Problem-Solving approach, do you think the parties would have achieved more efficient terms?

SINGLEPART/LARGECORP. EFFICIENCY POINTS

	SINGLEPART	*LARGECORP*
PRICE	+1/$20,000 over $7.5 mill.	-1/$20,000 $8.5-10 mill.
	-5/$10,000 under $7.5 mill.	-5/$10,000 over $10 mill.
$8.5 mill.:	+50 Singlepart	0 Largecorp
	[+1 & -1 per $20,000 from $8.5 mill. to $10 mill.]	
NONCOMPET.	No Non-Comp. Cl. +25	If no cl. of at least 2 yrs. -25
	Up to 3 Yr. Limit +15	Between 2-5 yrs. +20 **plus**
		10/yr. Over 2 yrs.
	Over 3 yrs. -10/yr. Over 3	5 Yr. Non-Comp. Cl. +75
5 yr. Cl.	-20 Singlepart	+75 Largecorp
EMPLOYEE	5 yr. Contract and Same	No Guarantees +40
GUARANTEES	Work Grps. +100	
	5 yr. Contract/Changed	Up to 3 yr. Guarantee 0
	Grps. +50	
	Guarantee Less than 5 yrs.	Guarantee over 3 yrs. -10/yr.
	(Same or Changed Grps.) 2	Over 3
	yrs. +20; 3 yrs. +30; 4 yrs.	
	+40	
	Guarantee less than 2 yrs.	Restriction on Work Grps.
	-50	-20
Same Grps. 5 Yr.	+100 Singlepart	-40 [-20 & -20]
Term		
WARRANTY/	*No Known Problems 0	No Known Problems +25
INDEMNIF.		
	No Known/Unknown -75	No Known/Unknown +50
	*Indemnif. up to 2 yrs. -30	*Indemnif. for 2 yrs. +50
	Indemnif. over 2 yrs. -100	Indemnif. for 5 yrs. +75
	*Liq. Dam. up to $150k -10	*Liq. Dam. of $100k +30
	Liq. Dam. over $150k -50	
CLOSING DATE	5 /mo. Up to 6 mo. Delayed	-8/mo. Delayed past 3 mo.
		-25/mo. Delayed past 6 mo.
3 Mo. Delay	+15 Singlepart	0 Largecorp

Chapter 8
IMPACT OF PROCESS ON POST-NEGOTIATION FEELINGS

Readers should divide into pairs. Each pair gets $10,000 that can be divided between the two persons. One participant should propose a division of the $10,000 to her partner — how much she would get and how much her partner would get. Once this division has been proposed, — with absolutely no discussion between the participants — the other party can either accept the proposed split — with each person receiving the allotted amount — or reject the proposed division — with neither person receiving anything.

After the initial exchange, the roles of the participants should be reversed. The person who was the recipient of the proposed division during the first round gets to propose a division between himself and his partner during this stage. His partner must either accept or reject the suggested division of the money.

When the participants have completed both iterations, they should consider how many suggested $5000/$5000 divisions, $6000/$4000 divisions, $7000/$3000 divisions, $8000/$2000 divisions, and $9000/$1000 divisions. They should determine how many of these different proposed splits were accepted by their recipients and how many were rejected.

When individuals engage in bargaining interactions, their perceptions concerning the fairness of the process can be critical.[1] Many persons are more satisfied with objectively less beneficial terms when they feel they were treated fairly and respectfully than with objectively more beneficial terms when they feel they were treated disrespectfully. This factor helps to explain why lawyers consider far more Cooperative/Problem-Solvers to be effective negotiators than Competitive/Adversarials. When they interact with members of the latter group, the offensive behavior by such persons causes them to dislike the entire process, regardless of the actual terms they obtain. It would also suggest why hybrid Competitve/Problem-Solvers employ a style that enables them to seek results that are most beneficial for their own side while inducing their opponents to think the process has been fair and that the different items have been equitably divided.

Some individuals suggest a $5000/$5000 division, and this offer is quickly accepted by their partners. Others propose a $6000/$4000 split favoring themselves. Most of their partners accept this division, believing that $4000 is better than nothing. A few, however, reject this proposal because they do not believe it is fair for the proposer to obtain a $2000 advantage. Some offer a $7000/$3000 split. Only about half of the offerees accept this proposal. Those who accept the $3000 do so reluctantly, because they think they have been unfairly short-changed. A few suggest an $8000/$2000 division — or even a $9000/$1000 split. These offers are usually rejected, due to their one-sided nature. The few people who accept these proposed divisions rationalize that

---

[1] *See* Rebecca Hollander-Blumoff, *Just Negotiation*, 88 Wash. U. L. Rev. 381 (2010); Rebecca Hollander-Blumoff & Tom Tyler, *Procedural Justice in Negotiation: Procedural Fairness, Outcome Acceptance, and Integrative Potential*, 33 Law & Soc. Inquiry 473 (2008).

$2000 or $1000 is preferable to nothing, even though they are angry at the unfair way they have been treated.

When the partners reverse their roles, those who were originally offered $5000/$5000 splits by their partners almost always offer similar 50/50 divisions which are expeditiously accepted. Those who were offered less generous divisions almost always offer their partners similarly unbalanced splits — and some offer their partners less generous divisions. For example. Individuals initially offered $6000/$4000 divisions respond with $7000/$3000 offers of their own.

When this exercise is finished, participants should appreciate the importance of giving negotiating opponents the sense they are being treated fairly. This concept is especially critical when negotiators possess greater bargaining power than their opponents and have the capacity to dictate the final terms to be agreed upon. They should try to provide the other side with sufficient benefits to induce them to think they are being treated equitably. Less important items should be conceded in return for more important terms, even if they might have been able to retain one or two of the issues being exchanged. If they fail to do this, they may discover that their opponents would rather generate mutual destruction through nonsettlements than to give in to agreements they think treat them inequitably.

Individuals should never gloat at the conclusion of bargaining interactions no matter how well they think they have done. Firstly, they may not have done as well as they think they have, and they will only embarrass themselves. Secondly, even if they have really out-performed the other side, they should realize how important it is to let the other side feel it was treated fairly. If that party develops "buyer's remorse," it may try to get out of the deal. This can become a costly mistake. Even if the other side decides to honor the one-sided arrangement, they will remember how negatively they were treated. When the parties meet again, they will be out for revenge. They will be like the students who were initially offered unequal divisions of the $10,000, and they will probably respond with their own efforts to get even.

When negotiators represent parties with on-going relationships, they should always appreciate the appearance of fairness. Parties that take advantage of short-term power imbalances will find their clients adversely affected by future power imbalances favoring the other side. Even when people are negotiating on behalf of parties unlikely to ever interact with these opponents again, the negotiators should appreciate the fact that the attorneys may interact again. This is especially true for lawyers who practice in certain geographical areas or specialize in relatively narrow disciplines. They will regularly encounter the same opponents in future settings involving different clients. Those advocates who take unfair advantage of these persons now will encounter much fiercer opposition in their future dealings than they would if they left those individuals with the sense they were being treated fairly and respectfully in their current encounters.

Chapter 9
NONVERBAL COMMUNICATION

Nonverbal communication, which is one of the most significant sources of information available to negotiators, is often overlooked. The negotiating parties tend to concentrate on what is being verbally communicated, and they fail to appreciate the information being nonverbally displayed. This is especially true when opponents are talking, but it is even true when these persons are speaking. Since most individuals find it easier to be less than forthright verbally than nonverbally, people who fail to observe opponent nonverbal signs are likely to miss the most trustworthy messages being communicated by their adversaries. Certain nonverbal signals may also suggest that accompanying verbal messages are deceitful. While no one signal is a conclusive indication of deception, observers who look for relevant nonverbal patterns and behavioral changes can learn to spot likely prevarication.

When individuals interact with others, they should watch them carefully and attempt to establish benchmarks for their behavior. How do they regularly move their hands, their arms, their legs, their head, and their gross body movement? What are their common facial expressions? Once they establish such benchmarks, they should look for **patterns of behavior** and for **changes in behavior** which may provide them with important information.

Skilled negotiators need to appreciate the importance of nonverbal signals. They should occasionally read books on this critical subject and watch body language being communicated by others in different settings.[1] The more attuned negotiators are to these subtle messages, the more they will appreciate the actual feelings of the people with whom they interact. Recognizing that it is difficult to simultaneously speak and watch the nonverbal responses of others, many negotiators take colleagues with them to look for such signals while they are talking.

It would be impossible to cover the many nonverbal signals explored in the many excellent books devoted to nonverbal communication, but it would be helpful to focus on a few to introduce readers the this critical topic. Once people begin to appreciate the importance of reading nonverbal signals, they may be induced to peruse several of these books in an effort to become more adept at reading such signs.

I. COMMON NONVERBAL SIGNALS

A. Facial Expressions

Facial expressions are the most easily manipulated forms of nonverbal communication for most persons, yet subtle clues to the actual feelings of the signalers can often be perceived by careful observers. Taut lips may indicate frustration or anxiety. A subtle smile, often hidden quickly by a bowed head, or brief signs of relief around the corners of opponent mouths when new offers are made, may indicate that the offeror has approached or entered the other side's settlement range.

---

[1] *See, e.g.*, Henry H. Calero, The Power of Nonverbal Communication (2005); Peter A. Anderson, The Complete Idiot's Guide to Body Language (2004); Susan Quilliam, Body Language (2004); Desmond Morris, Bodytalk (1994); Jo-Ellen Dimitrius & Mark Mazzarella, Reading People (1998).

B.   Flinch

A flinch may be an uncontrolled response to an inadequate offer or concession. This may sincerely indicate the unacceptable nature of the offer being conveyed. Manipulative negotiators may employ a contrived "flinch" to silently challenge the adequacy of opponent opening offers or concessions. Negotiators who encounter what they consider to be truly reactive flinches should decide if their announced positions are clearly unacceptable. On the other hand, negotiators who think opponents are using contrived flinches to induce them to bid against themselves with consecutive position changes should: (1) recognize the manipulative nature of their opponents and (2) be careful not to change positions until they have obtained position changes from their adversaries.

C.   Wringing of Hands

This is frequently a sign of frustration or tension. Distraught individuals often twist their hands and fingers into seemingly painful contortions. This signal usually emanates from persons who are anxious regarding aggressive tactics being employed by opponents or about wholly unsatisfactory negotiation developments.

D.   Rubbing Hands Together in Anticipatory Manner

This behavior is often exhibited by anxious negotiators who anticipate new and/or more beneficial offers from their opponents. Such conduct suggests an over-eagerness that may be satisfied with a minimal position change.

E.   Tightly Gripping Arm Rests/Drumming Fingers on Table

Impatient or frustrated persons frequently grip the arm rests of their chairs tightly or drum their fingers on the table. Negotiators who exhibit such behavior are most likely displeased with the lack of progress they think is occurring.

F.   Biting Lower Lip/Running Fingers Through Hair

These signals usually indicate stress or frustration. They emanate from persons who are disappointed by the lack of negotiation progress and/or their perceived opponent intransigence.

G.   Eyes Wandering/Looking at Watch

These are signs of boredom and disinterest. Such signals would suggest a serious lack of interest in what is being said. Negotiators who encounter such signs should ask their opponents questions to force them to become more involved in the substantive discussions.

H.   Opening Mouth But Not Speaking

This is usually a sign of indecision. This person would like to talk — and may even be contemplating a position change — but she is not yet sure of what to say. Opponents who encounter such a situation should remain silent and be patient. They need to give this person the time she needs to decide exactly what to say.

I.   Sitting on the Edge of One's Chair

This is a definite sign of interest. When it follows a newly articulated position, it suggests real interest in what is being offered. Most people do not actually sit on the front of their chair, but only lean slightly forward. On the other hand, some individuals lean so far forward they place their elbows on the table in front of them.

J.   Hands Touching Face/Stroking Chin/Playing with Glasses

These are signs of contemplation. Individuals feel uncomfortable sitting in silence while they consider unanticipated opponent disclosures or position changes. To cover their pregnant pauses, the actors use these devices to look as if something is actually happening while they contemplate their next moves. Such actors are likely to reject the offers that generated such nonverbal responses, but they will probably do so more positively to keep the process moving.

K.   Steepling (Hands Pressed Together with Hands or Fingers Pointed Upward)

This is a sign of confidence, suggesting that the actors are pleased with developments. Negotiators who observe such signals should be careful not to concede more than they have to.

L.   Leaning Back with Hands Behind Head

This particularly masculine posture is another sign of confidence. It may alternatively be an indication of contentedness. The actors are very pleased with negotiation developments. When men are interacting with women, it can also be a sign of domination. Female negotiators who observe such behavior in opponents should be cautious, because their opponents probably think things are going their way.

M.   Placing One Hand Behind Head

When individuals use one hand to clasp the neck behind their ears, this is usually an indication of distress. It is as if the actors are psychologically giving themselves consoling hugs to counteract the negative consequences they are experiencing. Negotiators exhibiting this posture most likely see negative developments ahead.

N.   Open/Uplifted Hands with Palms Facing Out

This posture is used to indicate the sincerity of what is being verbally communicated. It is frequently associated with "final offers" to demonstrate that the offeror has nothing more to concede. If the signal seems insincere, it is most likely a deliberate attempt to deceive opponents.

O.   Crossed Arms/Crossed Legs

This may be an aggressive, adversarial posture or a defensive position, depending on the particular position of the arms and legs. If the arms are folded high on the chest and the ankle of one leg is placed on the knee of the other leg, this tends to be a combative posture. On the other hand, if the arms are folded low on the chest and one leg is draped over the other, it is a more defensive posture. In both cases, however, these tend to be unreceptive positions. If opponents begin bargaining interactions in such positions, it can be beneficial to take the time to establish sufficient rapport to induce them to become more receptive to what is being discussed. When negotiators approach impasse, one or both often exhibit this posture.

P. Covering and Rubbing One Eye

This is a nonverbal sign of disbelief. It is the nonverbal equivalent of the disbelieving expression "my eye." Negotiators who encounter this posture when they are making critical representations should recognize the possibility their statements are not being accorded much respect. They may have to restate their communications in a more credible manner.

II. NONVERBAL SIGNS OF DECEPTION

In his classic book *Telling Lies* (1992), Paul Ekman noted that most people are unable to determine from nonverbal signals when they are being lied to. Some of this is due to the fact that dishonesty can range from mere puffing to unequivocal deceit. Despite the fact that no particular nonverbal sign is a certain indication of deception, there are some signals that should cause observers to become suspicious. Some reflect the stress usually associated with lying, while others are deliberately employed by speakers to enhance the credibility of the misrepresentations they are about to utter. No one signal should be assumed to indicate deception. Persons should look for changes in established behavior and patterns of behavior.[2]

A. Increase/Decrease in Statement Specificity

When individuals tell the truth, they fill in little details as they are recalled. When people lie, however, there are no actual details to remember. As a result, they often omit the usual amplifying details, articulating the bare bones of their fabrication. On the other hand, carefully prepared liars may provide an excessive amount of information designed to make their fabrications appear more credible. Specific questions can be used to force minimal detail liars to fill in details they do not really know or to discover whether detailed statements are really accurate.

B. Increased/Decreased Gross Body Movement

When individuals interact, they move their arms, legs, and torso regularly. They rarely sit perfectly still. Under stressful situations, some persons become more fidgety and move their arms and legs at an increased rate. Deceitful people who are afraid of getting caught may exhibit similar movement. On the other hand, some fabricators deliberately minimize their body movements in an effort to appear more trustworthy. As a result, negotiators should be on guard when they evaluate the veracity of statements emanating from individuals who have clearly increased or decreased their gross body movements.

---

[2] *See generally* ALDERT VRIJ, DETECTING LIES AND DECEIT (2000); DAVID J. LIEBERMAN, NEVER BE LIED TO AGAIN (1998); CHARLES V. FORD, LIES! LIES!! LIES!!! (1996).

C.   Placing Hand Over Mouth

Most persons believe that lying is morally wrong. Their consciences bother them when they deceive others. Psychologists have noticed that liars frequently place their hands over their mouths when they speak, as if they are subconsciously trying to hold in the lies they know are morally reprehensible.

D.   Eyes Looking Up to Wrong Side

When people try to *recall past circumstances* from memory, right handed individuals tend to look up and to the left and left handed persons tend to look up and to the right. On the other hand, when individuals try to *create new images*, right handed persons tend to look up and to the right and left handed people look up and to the left. When right handed negotiators look up and to the right or left handed negotiators look up and to the left, this may suggest that they are not trying to recall actual circumstances but are instead creating false stories.

E.   Dilated Pupils/More Frequent Blinking

When persons experience stress, the pupils of their eyes widen and their rate of blinking increases. Although negotiators rarely interact with others in such proximity that they can see the size of their pupils, they can easily notice increased blinking. This may be due to foreign matter that has entered the eyes of such people, or it may be due to stress associated with deception.

F.   Narrowing/Tightening of Margin of Lips

Stress often causes individuals to briefly narrow and tighten the red margin of their lips just before they speak. Careful observers may be able to see the lips of prospective speakers tighten into a narrow line across their lips just before they utter false statements.

G.   Elevated Voice Pitch

Persons experiencing anxiety frequently speak with an elevated voice pitch. Even though experienced prevaricators work to control their voice when they talk, listeners can often discern their higher voice pitch.

H.   More Deliberate/Rapid Speech

Individuals who experience stress when they lie may inadvertently speak more rapidly. On the other hand, persons who wish to have their misrepresentations completely heard may deliberately speak more slowly.

I.   Increased Speech Errors

Many persons who try to deceive others have a greater number of speech errors. They may stutter, repeat phrases, or trail off without finishing their statements. They may also include non-substantive modifiers like "you know" or "don't you think." It is as if their conscience is disrupting the communication between their brain and their mouth to prevent the prevarication.

J. More Frequent Clearing of Throat

The tension associated with lying may cause speakers to engage in more throat clearing. As they prepare to utter their false statements, they nervously clear their throats.

REVIEW OF NEGOTIATION VIDEO

Readers should view — either individually or in a group setting — one of the on-line negotiation videos available on the LexisNexis Web Course (Sexual Harassment Exercise or Peterson v. Denver Exercise). The first time they view the interaction, they should turn the sound off and merely look at what they see visually. They should try to determine how the interaction is developing. Which person seems more anxious or calm, more or less confident? Can they tell when position changes are being articulated? Does one party appear to be doing better than the other side? They should then watch the video with the sound on to see if their visual interpretations are consistent or inconsistent with what was actually occurring.

A second video available on the LexisNexis Web Course provides a graphic demonstration of many of the nonverbal signals described in this chapter.

Chapter 10
DEALING WITH ZERO-SUM EXERCISES

Practicing attorneys — and even law students — must occasionally negotiate with each other in cases in which the only issue is money and the amount agreed upon has to be paid now. These are classic *"zero-sum"* interactions, since each dollar obtained by one side constitutes a dollar lost by the other side. What makes these encounters difficult concerns the absence of different-value items the parties can use to expand the overall pie and jointly enhance their respective returns. These are thus classic competitive endeavors.

Readers should be paired and spend thirty to forty-five minutes working on the following ***Peterson v. Denver Exercise*** in which the only issue is money. The negotiators should ask themselves whether they find it more difficult or easier to negotiate problems that only involve the payment of money. Some may like the simplicity of such zero-sum exercises, while others may prefer multi-issue exercises which allow the parties to trade items they value less than their opponents for items they value more than their adversaries. By the conclusion of the term, most negotiators tend to express a preference for multi-item interactions which give them the opportunity to expand the pie and efficiently divide the non-zero-sum items before they have to deal with the zero-sum monetary issue.

GENERAL INFORMATION — PETERSON v. DENVER

At approximately 11:30 p.m. on a rainy and dark Friday evening last November, accountant Jim Denver was driving his Continental up Powell Street in San Francisco. He had just completed a long and acrimonious dinner meeting with a difficult, but important, client. Although he had consumed three or four Martinis during the course of his lengthy discussions, he felt in complete control of his faculties when he concluded the meeting.

As a result of the emergency session with his client, Denver was forced to miss a prestigious social event that his wife had been eagerly anticipating. He realized she would be very angry over the situation, and he was in a great hurry to return home to assuage her feelings. As Denver was heading up a particularly steep portion of Powell Street, he swerved toward the middle of the road to avoid a double-parked car, and he drove precariously close to an oncoming cable car on which Norma Peterson was riding.

Denver's mind was on both the problems with his client and his wife's ire, and he did not see Peterson, who was clumsily dismounting from the cable car in front of him. Peterson slipped on the wet pavement into the path of Denver's automobile, and she was directly struck before Denver could even apply his brakes.

Peterson suffered a broken back resulting in paralysis from the waist down. She was 40 years old at the time of the mishap. Peterson, who was a successful patent attorney at the time of the accident with Denver, has adapted herself well to her present condition and she is currently able to conduct her business as effectively as ever. However, one month ago, her husband instituted marital dissolution proceedings. She contends that this was brought on by her paralyzed condition.

Peterson has sued Denver for $5,000,000. Her medical expenses and lost earnings total about $250,000. The State of California is a comparative negligence jurisdiction. Any settlement figure agreed upon must be paid to Peterson immediately.

CONFIDENTIAL INFORMATION — PETERSON ATTORNEYS

CONFIDENTIAL INFORMATION — PETERSON ATTORNEYS

You are aware that on the night of the accident, Peterson had been drinking heavily at a bar with a favorite male associate from her office. She had not intended to leave the cable car where she did, but, in her intoxicated state, had fallen off the car and slipped on the wet pavement into the path of Denver's automobile. Nevertheless, you have located an apparently reliable witness who is positive that Denver was speeding and swerving sharply at the moment he struck Peterson. You have suspicions that Denver may have consumed several drinks too many before he commenced his drive home, but you have not been able to substantiate this fact.

You have been informed that Mr. Peterson had been planning to dissolve his marriage prior to the accident due to his wife's extra-marital affairs, and you know that her injury did not precipitate this action. In fact, Peterson's disability may have precluded his filing for dissolution at an earlier time.

Peterson, who is reputed to be a solid citizen, is terrified of the adverse consequences that might be caused to her lucrative practice should her clients learn of her drinking and "dating" proclivities. She has thus decided *not* to press her suit against Denver to trial. She would like to recover at least $250,000 to cover her medical expenses and lost earnings, and would be pleased to recover any amount above that figure. She is presently earning $175,000 per year.

Since Peterson does not wish to take this case to trial, you will automatically be placed at the **bottom** of Plaintiff groups if you fail to reach any agreement. If you achieve a settlement, your group placement will be determined by the amount of money Peterson is to receive.

CONFIDENTIAL INFORMATION — DENVER ATTORNEYS

CONFIDENTIAL INFORMATION — DENVER ATTORNEYS

You know that your client had been drinking on the night in question, but you doubt that this adversely influenced his driving ability. However, you suspect that he was driving too fast for such a damp and dark night on busy Powell Street. You also realize that Denver's mind was on his client and wife at the moment it should have been concentrating on the traffic, and you believe that a jury could conclude that he had driven negligently.

You have learned of the excellent reputation which Peterson has in the community, and you have been led to believe that her paralysis has caused her husband to sue for dissolution after 15 years of apparently blissful marriage. You have discovered from investigation that Peterson had visited a bar with one of her male associates prior to the time she had boarded the cable car on Powell Street, but she has stated that she had only stopped off after work to help him celebrate his birthday. She has denied any heavy drinking. Although you believe that she had been out quite late to have merely been engaged in a friendly birthday celebration, you have no hard evidence to refute Peterson's story.

Your client is worried about the effect any adverse publicity could have on his business, and he would like to settle the case as soon as possible. Denver has a $1,000,000 automobile insurance policy, and has the personal assets to cover an additional $1,000,000. The insurance carrier has authorized you to pay the entire $1,000,000 policy limit, and Denver has said that he is willing to provide an additional $1,000,000 cash, if necessary. He is hoping, however, that you will be able to settle this matter within the scope of his insurance coverage.

If you reach a settlement, your group placement will be determined by the amount of money you agree to pay to Peterson. If you do not achieve any settlement, you will be treated as if you lost a $2,000,000 judgment, with that $2,000,000 figure being used to determine your group placement.

SELF-ASSESSMENT

SELF-ASSESSMENT

When the negotiators have completed their exercise, the different results should be compared. In most cases, the results vary widely. Some claimants established elevated aspiration levels and obtained highly beneficial results for their side, while other claimants established more modest goals and obtained less beneficial results. The same is true for the party having to pay money. Individuals who thought they should not have to pay much usually agree to pay less than those who thought they would have to pay more. This aspect of the exercise reinforces the notion that there is a direct correlation between negotiator aspiration levels and final outcomes.

Settlements usually range from about $200,000 to $2,000,000. Denver representatives occasionally agree to sums in excess of $2,000,000, even though that is all they would have to pay if no settlement is achieved. This demonstrates the pressure some negotiators feel to achieve agreements, even if the agreements reached are worse than what would occur if no accord was agreed upon.

When participants discuss the settlements reached in the $200,000 to $300,000 or the $1,900,000 to $2,000,000 ranges, they should appreciate the fact that as parties approach their **own bottom lines** they tend to feel **greater pressure** to **reach agreements** when they should actually feel less pressure. As Denver representatives approach the $2,000,000 figure, they have little to lose from nonsettlements. They will only have to pay the $2,000,000 assigned to them if no agreement is achieved. On the other hand, the Peterson representatives will fall from the elevated positions being considered to the bottom of their group. It is thus most unlikely that Peterson representatives would ever walk away from $1,500,000, $1,750,000, or $1,900,000 offers. The same phenomenon occurs with respect to Peterson representatives debating whether to accept offers in the $200,000 to $300,000 range. They have to appreciate the fact they are going to end up with very low results. If they consider their opponent's situations, they should realize that their opponents have more to lose from nonsettlements than they do. In fact, the Denver representatives would fall from the current areas being discussed to $2,000,000.

Participants should consider ways in which to turn zero-sum negotiations into non-zero-sum interactions. Does the injured person want to obtain an apology from the responsible party? Does the payer wish to obtain a non-admission clause that will allow her client to save face by denying actual liability? Do one or both sides wish a confidentiality provision that will prevent public disclosure of the matter being resolved? Would both parties benefit from a structured settlement that would involve future payments? Would the claimant benefit from in-kind payments, such as a promise to repair something that has been damaged or a promise to take care of an injured person's future medical treatment? What other issues might the parties consider in ways that would enhance their ability to achieve mutually beneficial resolutions of their matters?

Chapter 11
IMPACT OF ANCHORING ANCHORING EXERCISE

ANCHORING EXERCISE

Three months ago, Sarah Plaintiff was driving down Main Street toward First Street. As she approached the Third Street intersection, a car turned in front of her causing her to brake. Her car slowed from 35 mph to 10 mph. Charlie Defendant was driving behind Plaintiff. He was talking on his cell phone and failed to see the brake lights on Plaintiff's car. As a result, he failed to slow down until the last moment, causing him to strike the rear end of Plaintiff's car at 35 mph.

Ms. Plaintiff sustained a whiplash injury to her neck. She has continuing pain for which she takes pain medication, and still has to wear a neck brace. If her condition does not improve in the near future, minimally invasive surgery may have to be performed to lessen her discomfort. It cost Plaintiff $7500 to have the rear end of her car repaired.

You represent Defendant. This week, you received a settlement proposal from Plaintiff's attorney demanding $100,000 to cover the car repairs, the pain and suffering Plaintiff has suffered and continues to experience, and the cost of neck surgery if that becomes necessary.

You have to prepare for your negotiation with Plaintiff's attorney.

(A)   What would be the ***first offer*** you would make to Plaintiff's attorney:

$_____

(B)   How much do you think you will finally ***have to pay*** Plaintiff to resolve this claim?

$_____

Suppose the Plaintiff's demand letter you just received asked for $50,000.

(A)   What would be the **first offer** you would make in response to this demand:

    $_____

(B)   How much do you think you will finally **have to pay** the Plaintiff now to resolve this claim:

    $_____

SELF-ASSESSMENT

SELF-ASSESSMENT

Most respondents initially offered much more in response to the $100,000 demand than the $50,000 demand. Some may have even offered more than $50,000. They also expected to pay more in response to the higher figure than the lower figure — some in the $50,000 range. Their planned opening offers and settlement goals are reduced significantly in response to the $50,000 Plaintiff demands. They then begin to appreciate the true impact of ***anchoring***, as they realize the degree to which their own planned responses to Plaintiff opening offers were significantly influenced by the specific amounts being sought by those parties.

When individuals prepare for bargaining interactions, they should appreciate the impact of anchoring. They should realize that less generous opening offers are likely to induce opponents to think they will do less well than they anticipated, causing those persons to reduce their expectations. On the other hand, more generous offers are likely to embolden their opponents by inducing them to think they will achieve better results than they anticipated.

As readers work on other negotiation exercises, they should compare opening offers/demands with final terms agreed upon to see whether less generous offers/demands tend to generate more advantageous terms than more generous offers/demands.

Chapter 12
IMPACT OF PSYCHOLOGICAL FACTORS

I. GAIN-LOSS FRAMING

Suppose you had to choose between the following options. Which would you select?

1. I will give you a $100 bill.
2. I will give you a sealed envelope. Four out of five will be empty; one out of five will contain five $100 bills.

About 90 percent of individuals select Option 1 to obtain the sure $100.

What if you had to select from the following options.

1. You have to pay me $100.
2. Four out of five do not have to pay me anything, but one out of five has to pay me $500.

About 90 percent decide to take their chances with Option 2 in an effort to avoid having to pay me anything.

Why do most of the persons offered $100 or a one-in-five chance of getting $500 select the sure $100, while most of the individuals who either have to pay $100 or face a one-in-five chance of paying $500 take their chances on the one-in-five alternative? The answer is *gain-loss framing*.[1] Persons who have to choose between a *sure gain* and the possibility of obtaining a greater gain or no gain tend to be *risk averse*. They want to obtain something for sure, and they opt for the certain gain. Individuals who must choose between a *sure loss* and the possibility of a greater loss or no loss tend to be *risk takers*. They select the option that gives them the opportunity to suffer no loss.

How does *gain-loss framing* influence bargaining interactions? Negotiators who must choose between sure gains and the possibility of greater gains or no gains tend to be risk averse and they select the sure gains. On the other hand, negotiators who must choose between sure losses and the possibility of greater losses or no losses tend to be risk takers and they opt for the possibility of no losses. When transactional negotiators are debating whether to buy or sell a company or commercial real estate, or to license software, any decision they make tends to look like a gain. As a result both the potential buyer or seller or licensor or licensee tend to be risk averse. This factor increases the likelihood they will reach a mutually beneficial agreement. Neither wants to leave the interaction empty-handed.

When litigators are trying to resolve a legal dispute, however, gain-loss framing tends to have a different impact on claimants compared to defendants. Plaintiffs and their attorneys — who are usually being compensated on a contingent fee basis — have to choose between the sure gain being offered them by defendants and the possibility of greater gains or no gains offered by trial alternatives. Both claimants and their attorneys thus tend to be risk averse and accept the certain gains being offered to them over the mere possibility of greater results at trial. Defendants, on the other hand, have to choose between what they view as sure losses and the

---

[1] *See* Chris Guthrie, *Prospect Theory, Risk Preference, and the Law*, 97 Nw. L. Rev. 1115, 1117–27 (2003); Chris Guthrie, Jeffrey J. Rachlinski & Andrew J. Wistrich, *Inside the Judicial Mind*, 86 Cornell L. Rev. 777, 794–99 (2001).

possibility of greater losses or no losses if they go to trial. They tend to be risk takers hoping to avoid any losses. How can plaintiff representatives diminish the impact of this phenomenon? They can try to frame their demands as if they are "gains" to the defendants. They can suggest that for the amount of money they are requesting, the defendant problems will be resolved. If they can induce defendants to view their offers as providing them with gains, the defendants will become more risk averse — and become more inclined to accept the amounts being requested.

II.   OPTIMISTIC OVER-CONFIDENCE

Arturo Plaintiff and Dianne Defendant reside in a traditional contributory negligence jurisdiction. One day, Plaintiff is driving down Oak Street while talking on his cell phone. Defendant is driving up Oak Street while text messaging a friend on her blackberry. Both are distracted by their cell phone operations, and they cross over into the center part of the street. Before either has the opportunity to take evasive action, the left front portion of their vehicles collide causing several thousand dollars of damage to both of their cars. Plaintiff also sustains a broken left arm and lacerations to his face. Defendant sustains no personal injuries at all. Plaintiff has sued Defendant in State Court seeking compensation for the damage to his vehicle and to himself.

Readers should divide themselves into two groups. One group should be designated "Plaintiffs" and the other "Defendants." They should be asked two questions:

1.   What is the probability Plaintiff will prevail if this case goes to trial?

2.   What is the likely monetary result if Plaintiff prevails at trial?

The individuals designated "Plaintiffs" tend to **over-estimate** both the probability Plaintiff will prevail at trial *and* the likely monetary result if Plaintiff does prevail. The persons designated "Defendants," however, tend to **under-estimate** both the probability Plaintiff will prevail at trial *and* the likely monetary result if Plaintiff does prevail.

Individuals tend to evaluate likelihood outcomes from their *own perspective*. Persons designated "Plaintiffs" put themselves in the shoes of Plaintiff when assessing the likely trial outcomes, and they over-estimate both the probability Plaintiff will prevail and the likely monetary outcome. Persons designated "Defendants" do just the opposite, under-estimating the probability Plaintiff will prevail and the likely monetary result. This *optimistic over-confidence*[2] has nothing to do with whether individuals are actually plaintiffs — or their attorneys — or defendants — or their attorneys. It is a natural psychological factor that can influence anyone. How does this factor influence dispute resolution negotiations? It tends to induce claimants to over-estimate the value of their claims and defendants to under-estimate the value of plaintiff claims. How can the gap between these different perspectives be closed? Through the impact of transaction costs. Plaintiffs have to *subtract* anticipated transaction costs from their predicted trial results, while defendants have to *add* anticipated transaction costs to their predicted results. This factor thus reduces the plaintiff's anticipated outcomes at the same time it increases the defendant's anticipated outcomes.

---

[2] *See* Russell Korobkin, *Psychological Impediments to Mediation Success*, 21 Ohio St. J. Disp. Res. 281, 284–98 (2006).

III.   ENDOWMENT EFFECT

Half the participants should be informed that they have just received insulated coffee mugs with a retail value of $10. The other half are not provided with anything. The individuals with the mugs should then be asked how much someone would have to pay them to purchase their mugs. Most will ask for $11 or $12 dollars. It is as if they have spent $10 to purchase their mugs, and they wish to make a profit. The persons without mugs should then be asked how much they would be willing to purchase a mug from one of their mug-possessing classmates. They tend to cite a figure in the $8 to $9 range. Why? Individuals who possess something being sought by someone else tend to over-value it, while persons who are thinking of purchasing something held by someone else tend to under-value it.

The impact of the ***endowment effect***[3] can be especially important for transactional negotiators who are thinking of buying or selling a business firm or commercial real estate. They should appreciate the fact that the sellers are likely to over-value their holdings, while the buyers under-value those assets. Neither side should be offended by this psychological tendency. To avoid a personal conflict, they should focus on the objective factors, instead of the subjective factors. How much is the business firm actually worth from a purely economic perspective? How much is the real property worth from a market-place perspective?

The impact of the ***endowment effect*** is likely to be especially pronounced where the property someone is trying to acquire was personally developed by the seller. That person remembers all of the work that went into developing the business or the commercial real estate, and the many nights and weekends she may have put in. Potential buyers do not place a value on such considerations — they are only concerned about the detached economic value of what they are thinking of buying. They should not, however, ignore the seller's personal investment. They should praise that person for her accomplishments with respect to the business or property, then shift the focus to the objective market value of the item being discussed. This approach respects the personal feelings of the seller, while simultaneously trying to induce that person to evaluate the situation in a more detached manner.

IV.   REGRET AVERSION

When people have to make decisions, they often act in ways that will enable them to avoid the likelihood they will subsequently discover that they made the incorrect present decision.[4] For example, if a plaintiff fails to accept a defendant settlement offer and obtains less beneficial results at trial, the plaintiff will have real regrets. If a businessperson rejects a current offer from a prospective purchaser and ultimately obtains a lesser amount for her business from a future buyer, she will regret not having accepted the former offer. How can individuals avoid such feelings of regret? They can act presently in ways that diminish the likelihood they will later discover that they made the wrong decision. If the plaintiff accepts a current defendant offer, there will be no subsequent trial and no clear indication that the present decision was

---

[3] *See* Russell Korobkin, *The Endowment Effect and Legal Analysis*, 97 Nw. U. L. Rev. 1227, 1227-35 (2003).

[4] *See* Chris Guthrie, *Better Settle than Sorry: The Regret Aversion Theory of Litigation Behavior*, 1999 U. Ill. L. Rev. 43.

incorrect. If the firm seller accepts the present offer, she is unlikely to be certain that waiting would have been the preferable course of action.

How can **regret aversion** be used by negotiators to encourage others to accept their offers? If the individuals making the offers subtly infer that rejection of their offers may cause the persons rejecting their offers to suffer regrets when they ultimately realize that these offers are the best they will get, this would encourage the offer recipients to give serious thought to accepting their outstanding offers. This would enable them to get on with their lives without having to deal with subsequent developments that prove that they made the wrong choice now.

As readers work on different negotiation exercises, they should contemplate the degree to which **gain-loss framing**, **optimistic over-confidence**, the **endowment effect**, or **regret aversion** may have influenced their bargaining interactions. To what degree were their own behaviors affected by any of these considerations? To what degree were their opponent's behaviors so affected? Did they do anything during their interactions to use these phenomena to generate opponent behaviors that would favorably impact their own side's results?

V. PARADOX OF CHOICE

In *The Paradox of Choice* (2004), Professor Barry Schwartz discusses how hard it is for most people to accurately evaluate the comparative value of many items. When persons only have three or four choices, they tend to compare all three or four together and select the one that best suits their needs. When they have ten, twenty, or thirty options, it is virtually impossible to compare them all at once. They thus break these items into groups of four or five and make a series of separate comparisons. They select one from the first group, another from the second group, and so on. When they are done with this process, they should compare all of the items they have selected from the different groups and objectively assess their relative values. People often do not do this, however, due to the fact they tend to focus more on their most recent decisions than on their earlier determinations. Although the item they initially selected from the first comparative group would be best for them, they may actually select an item from the last or the next-to-last group, due to the fact it looked so good compared to the other items in those particular groups. Individuals thus fail to compare them neutrally with the first couple of items they chose from earlier groups.

When negotiators have many items to consider from options being offered by others, they may have to make their initial assessments on a group-by-group basis. When they are finished with these small group comparisons, they should be careful to put all of the selected items together in a single new group and compare them objectively with one another. They should try not to let their most recent small group determinations overly influence their final selection.

VI. ENTRAPMENT

If a number of individuals are present, one should act as the auctioneer and auction off a $1.00 bill. The auctioneer should announce that the bill will go to the highest bidder in exchange for her bid. But, unlike the usual auction, the *second highest bidder* will not get the bill but *will have to pay* his bid. The bidding has to begin at 50 cents to prevent someone from opening with a bid of $1.00 to end the auction. After someone bids 50 cents, others enter the auction hoping to make some money. As the bidding gets to 90 or 95 cents, the second highest bidder usually bids $1.00 hoping to break even. Once the new second highest bidder realizes that he will still have to pay 90 or 95 cents, he almost always bids $1.05 or $110, attempting to limit his loss. At this point, the $1.00 bidder usually increases her bid to $1.20 or $1.25 hoping to shut out the other bidder and allow her to minimize her loss. The bidding frequently reaches $1.50 to $1.75 before one of the bidders gives up.

The Dollar Auction graphically demonstrates a critical factor that affects many negotiators — **entrapment**. When people begin a negotiation, they hope to get a good deal. As they put more and more time into the bargaining process, they become entrapped — they want a deal even if it is no longer in their best interest. As a result, they agree to terms that are worse than their nonsettlement alternatives. Negotiators must always remember their nonsettlement options. When it becomes clear that the only accord they can obtain is worse, they should walk away with no agreement realizing that a nonsettlement is preferable to a bad deal. They have not wasted their time bargaining. They had to interact with the other side to determine if a beneficial arrangement could be achieved. Their efforts have provided them with critical information. They are better off with no accord.

When negotiators break off present talks, they should always do so pleasantly for two reasons. First, once the other side realizes that they are willing to walk away, it may decide to make them another offer. Second, even if this does not occur and the present discussions end, the parties are likely to see each other again and it is best not to adversely affect future talks with a negative parting of the ways now.

VII.   ATTRIBUTION BIAS

When beneficial things occur, people tend to overestimate the degree to which their own personal efforts ("dispositional characteristics") contributed to the results, but when negative things take place, individuals tend to underestimate their personal responsibility for those events attributing them to "situational characteristics" beyond their control.[5] For example, if defendants are involved in accidents or business disputes, they are likely to attribute the negative consequences to factors beyond their control. This phenomenon can anger the adversely affected parties who think the responsible persons are unfairly refusing to accept the blame for their actions. If individuals think their own actions have meaningfully contributed to negative results, they should at least minimally acknowledge their responsibility and offer sincere apologies to the persons adversely affected. This approach can diminish the emotional baggage that would otherwise fester in the harmed parties.

This "self-serving attribution bias" also becomes apparent in negotiation courses as students work on a series of negotiation exercises. As the term progresses, students who have performed well on the exercises attribute their success to personal characteristics such as intelligence, perseverance, and careful planning.[6] On the other hand, students who have not achieved good results tend to criticize the "unrealistic" exercises or blame their "uncooperative" or "unethical" opponents. This phenomenon makes it difficult for instructors to work with students who have not performed well to modify their behavior in ways that might improve their results. Since they blame external factors for their lack of success, it is not easy for them to accept the fact that some of their own attributes may be undermining their performance.

---

[5] *See* Deepak Malhotra & Max H. Bazerman, Negotiation Genius 135–36 (2007).

[6] *See id.* at 135.

Chapter 13
IMPACT OF GENDER ON NEGOTIATIONS

In *Women Don't Ask* (2003), Linda Babcock and Sara Laschever noted that in 2001 while 57 percent of male Carnegie Mellon graduate business students negotiated their starting salaries, only 7 percent of women did so — resulting in male starting salaries 7.6 percent higher than those obtained by women. Why don't women seek to negotiate as frequently as men? If they did so, is there any reason to think they would not do as well?[1]

When men and women negotiate with people of the opposite gender — and even the same gender — stereotypical beliefs influence their interactions. Many men and women assume that males are highly competitive, manipulative, win-lose negotiators who want to obtain good deals from their opponents. Females are considered more accommodating, win-win negotiators who seek to preserve existing relationships by maximizing the joint returns achieved by negotiating parties. If these stereotypical assumptions are correct, we might expect male lawyers and business persons to achieve better negotiating results than female attorneys and business persons.

I. REAL AND PERCEIVED GENDER-BASED DIFFERENCES

Men are thought to be rational and logical; women are considered emotional and intuitive. Men are expected to emphasize objective fact; women focus more on the maintenance of relationships. Men are expected to be dominant and authoritative; women are supposed to be passive and submissive. When men and women interact, males tend to speak for longer periods of time and to interrupt more often than women.[2] Men employ more direct language, while women often exhibit tentative and deferential speech patterns. If a man is hungry, he is likely to say: "I'm hungry, let's get something to eat." If a woman is hungry, she is likely to ask: "Are you hungry?" which should be interpreted to mean that she would like to get something to eat. During personal interactions, men are more likely than women to employ "highly intensive language" to persuade others, and they are more effective using this approach. Females tend to employ language containing more disclaimers ("I think"; "you know") than their male cohorts, which causes women to be perceived as less forceful. This gender-based factor is counterbalanced by the fact that women continue to be more sensitive to nonverbal signals than their male cohorts. As a result, they are more likely to be attuned to the subtle messages conveyed by opponents during bargaining encounters.

Gender-based stereotypes cause many people difficulty when they interact with attorneys and business people of the opposite gender.[3] Men often expect women to

---

[1] *See* LINDA BABCOCK & SARA LASCHEVER, ASK FOR IT (2008) (noting that with training in this regard, 68 percent of female Carnegie Mellon University business school graduates and 65 percent of male graduates negotiated their starting salaries in 2005, resulting in starting salaries for both groups 15 percent higher than for their cohorts who did not negotiate their starting salaries); *see also* Charles B. Craver, *If Women Don't Ask: Implications for Bargaining Encounters, the Equal Pay Act, and Title VII*, 102 MICH. L. REV. 1104 (2004).

[2] *See* DEBORAH TANNEN, TALKING FROM 9 TO 5, at 53-77 (1994).

[3] *See generally* Deborah Kolb, *More Than Just a Footnote: Constructing a Theoretical Framework for Teaching About Gender in Negotiation*, 16 NEGOT. J. 347 (2000); DEBORAH KOLB & JUDITH WILLIAMS, THE SHADOW NEGOTIATION (2000).

behave like "ladies" during their bargaining interactions. Overt aggressiveness that would be considered vigorous advocacy if employed by men may be characterized as offensive and threatening when used by women. This is especially true when females employ foul language and loud voices. Male negotiators who would immediately counter such tactics by other men with quid pro quo responses frequently find it difficult to adopt retaliatory approaches against women. When men permit such an irrelevant factor to influence and restrict their responsive behavior, they provide their female opponents with a bargaining advantage. Some men also find it difficult to act as competitively toward female opponents as they would toward male opponents. These men give further leverage to their female opponents.

Male attorneys and business people occasionally make the mistake of assuming that their female opponents will not engage in as many negotiating "games" as their male adversaries. Even many women erroneously assume that other females will not employ the Machiavellian tactics stereotypically associated with members of the competitive male culture. Men *and* women who expect their female adversaries to behave less competitively and more cooperatively often ignore the realities of their negotiation encounters and give a significant bargaining advantage to women who are willing to employ manipulative tactics.

Some male negotiators attempt to gain a psychological advantage against aggressive females by casting aspersions on the femininity of those individuals. They hope to embarrass those bargainers and make them feel self-conscious with respect to the approach they are using. Female negotiators should never allow adversaries to employ this tactic. They have the right to use any techniques they think appropriate, regardless of the stereotypes those tactics might contradict. To male opponents who raise specious objections to their otherwise proper conduct, they should reply that they do not wish to be viewed as "ladies," but merely as participants in bargaining interactions in which their gender should be irrelevant.

Women do not feel as comfortable in overtly competitive situations as their male colleagues. This factor may explain why a greater percentage of women (39%) take my Legal Negotiation course, in which final grades are influenced by performance on bargaining exercises, on a credit/no-credit basis than men (27%). Many women are apprehensive regarding the negative consequences they associate with competitive achievement, fearing that competitive success will alienate them from others. Males in my Legal Negotiation course tend to be more accepting of extreme results obtained by other men than by such results achieved by women. Even female students tend to be more critical of women who attain exceptional results than they are of men who do so. A number of males have privately admitted to me that they are also fearful of "losing" to female opponents, preferring the risk of non-settlements than the embarrassment of being defeated by women.

Males tend to exude more confidence than women in performance-oriented settings. Even when minimally prepared, men think they can "wing it" and get through successfully.[4] On the other hand, no matter how thoroughly prepared women are, they tend to feel unprepared.[5] I have often observed this difference among my Legal Negotiation students. Successful males think they can achieve beneficial results in future settings, while successful females continue to express doubts about their

---

[4] *See* Daniel Goleman, Working with Emotional Intelligence 7 (1998). *See generally* Peggy McIntosh, *Feeling Like a Fraud* (Wellesley Centers for Women 1985).

[5] *See* GAIL EVANS, PLAY LIKE A MAN, WIN LIKE A WOMAN 84–85 (2000).

own capabilities. I find this frustrating, because the accomplished women are as proficient as their accomplished male cohorts.

Male and female self-confidence is influenced by the stereotypical ways in which others evaluate their performances. When men are successful, their performance tends to be attributed to intrinsic factors such as hard work and intelligence; when women are successful, their performance is likely to be attributed to extrinsic factors such as luck or the assistance of others.[6] This factor causes male success to be overvalued, and female success to be undervalued.

Men and women often view appropriate bargaining outcomes differently. Women tend to prefer *equal exchanges*, while men tend to prefer *equitable exchanges*.[7] These beliefs may cause female negotiators to accept equal results even when they possess greater bargaining power than their opponents, while male negotiators seek equitable exchanges that reflect relevant power imbalances.

Gender-based competitive differences may be attributable to the different acculturation process for boys and girls.[8] Parents tend to be more protective of their daughters than their sons.[9] Most boys are exposed to competitive situations at an early age.[10] They have been encouraged to participate in little league baseball, basketball, football, soccer, and other competitive athletic endeavors. These activities introduce boys to the "thrill of victory and the agony of defeat" during their formative years. "Traditional girls' games like jump rope and hopscotch are turn-taking games, where competition is indirect since one person's success does not necessarily signify another's failure." While it is true that little league and interscholastic sports for women have become more competitive in recent years, most continue to be less overtly competitive than corresponding male athletic endeavors.[11]

II. STATISTICAL RESULTS

Since 1973, I have taught Legal Negotiation courses in which we study the negotiation process and the factors that influence bargaining interactions. My students engage in a series of bargaining exercises, the results of which affect their course grades. Over the past thirty-five years, I have performed several statistical analyses of student negotiation performance based upon gender.[12] I have found absolutely no statistically significant differences between the results achieved by men and by women. The average results are almost identical. Several people suggested to me that while the average results might be equal, the male results would be more

---

[6] *See* KAY DEAUX, THE BEHAVIOR OF WOMEN AND MEN 30–32 (1976).

[7] *See* ROY J. LEWICKI, JOSEPH A. LITTERER, JOHN W. MINTON & DAVID M. SAUNDERS, NEGOTIATION 330 (2d ed. 1994).

[8] *See* Carrie Menkel-Meadow, *Teaching About Gender and Negotiation: Sex, Truths, and Videotape*, 16 NEGOT. J. 357, 362–64 (2000).

[9] *See* NICKY MARONE, WOMEN AND RISK 42–45 (1992).

[10] *See* Evans, *supra* note 5, at 12–13.

[11] *See id.* at 80.

[12] *See* Charles B. Craver, *The Impact of Gender on Negotiation Performance*, 14 CARDOZO J. CONFLICT RES. __ (2013); Charles B. Craver, *Gender and Negotiation Performance*, 4 SOC. PRAC. 183 (2002); Charles B. Craver & David W. Barnes, *Gender, Risk Taking and Negotiation Performance*, 5 MICH. J. GENDER & LAW 299 (1999). *Compare* Russell Korobkin & Joseph Doherty, *Who Wins in Settlement Negotiations?*, 11 AMER. L. & ECON. REV. 162 (2009) (finding significant male bargaining advantage on single negotiation exercise conducted by first year law students with no negotiation training).

widely distributed. This theory was based upon the premise that women are more accommodating and less competitive, generating more results in the mid-range, while more competitive, win-lose males would either achieve highly beneficial results or well below average results. If this hypothesis were correct, the standard deviations for the more dispersed males would be higher than those for the centrally concentrated females. The fact that I have found no statistically significant differences with respect to the male and female standard deviations contradicts this theory.

Over the past thirty-five years, I have discovered that practicing attorneys and law students of both genders permit gender-based stereotypes to influence their negotiating interactions with persons of the opposite gender — and even people of the same gender. Many individuals assume that men are highly competitive, manipulative negotiators who always seek to obtain maximum results for themselves, while female negotiators are more accommodating and less competitive interactants who try to maximize the joint returns achieved by the parties.

Legal practitioners should acknowledge the impact that gender-based stereotypes may have upon negotiation interactions. Male attorneys who think that female opponents will not be as competitive or manipulative as their male colleagues provide women adversaries with an inherent advantage. They let their guards down and behave less competitively against female opponents than they would toward male opponents. Female negotiators must also reject gender-based stereotypical beliefs with respect to both male and female opponents. Women who conclude that adversaries are treating them less seriously because of their gender should not hesitate to take advantage of the situation. The favorable bargaining outcomes achieved by these women should teach chauvinistic opponents a crucial lesson.

Law firm managers should be careful to minimize the impart of gender stereotyping when they evaluate male and female performance. They should not over-value the success of men and under-value the success of women by attributing male accomplishment to intrinsic factors but female achievement to extrinsic factors. They should also try not to be critical of women whose negotiation styles would be viewed favorably if employed by males but negatively when used by women.

POST CHAPTER QUESTIONS

Readers should ask themselves if their own negotiation interactions may have been influenced by gender-related stereotypes.

(1) To what extend have their negotiation interactions confirmed or contradicted their gender-based expectations?

(2) Have their relationships with negotiation *partners* been affected by gender?

    (A) Who took the lead during negotiation encounters?

    (B) Which partner talked more during their negotiations?

    (C) Which partner took notes during their bargaining interactions?

(3) Have their relationships with negotiation *opponents* been affected by gender?

    (A) Eye contact while they are speaking/being spoken to?

    (B) Participants treating their ideas as more or less important?

(4) To what degree have they allowed their own gender-based assumptions/expectations to influence their interactions with others?

    (A) Do they feel more comfortable with a *partner* of the same gender or the opposite gender?

    (B) Do they feel more comfortable with *opponents* of the same gender or the opposite gender?

(5) Have they used the Preliminary Stage to develop better rapport with opponents of the opposite gender — especially when they thought the initial discussions may have been affected by gender-based stereotypes?

Participants should pair off and work on a negotiation exercise. Partnerships could include one male and one female against partnerships similarly divided, or the partnerships could be both male or both female, with male pairs negotiating with female pairs to see if negotiators think these pairings have affected their interactions with partners and/or opponents. After they have completed the exercise, they should explore the degree to which the gender of the participants may have affected their interactions.

Chapter 14
TELEPHONE AND E-MAIL NEGOTIATIONS

Many bargaining interactions between attorneys are conducted over the telephone or via e-mail due to the cost and time-consuming nature of in-person sessions. Even when lawyers have offices in the same metropolitan area, it would take too much time to take a taxi back and forth to each other's office. Quick telephone calls and e-mail exchanges are used to keep the negotiation process going. When attorneys are located in different cities, different states, or different countries, it would be impractical to conduct all of the necessary interactions on an in-person basis. Both telephone negotiations and e-mail negotiations can differ substantially from in-person interactions, yet most lawyers rarely think about the differences involved. As a result, they may place themselves at a distinct disadvantage vis-a-vis others who know how to use telephone and e-mail exchanges more proficiently.

I. TELEPHONE NEGOTIATIONS

Telephone interactions are less personal than in-person discussions. When face-to-face negotiations are conducted, the Preliminary Stage usually begins with some small talk to set the stage for the serious discussions that will follow. When one party phones another to discuss a particular situation, they are less likely to take the time to establish some rapport with the other side and to create a more positive bargaining environment — both of which enhance the likelihood of more cooperative behavior, a successful conclusion, and a more efficient exchange of terms.

Since telephone exchanges are less personal than face-to-face interactions, it is easier for participants to employ overtly competitive — and even openly adversarial — tactics. Many persons also find it easier to use deceptive tactics over the phone. Individuals tend to find it easier to reject offers being articulated by others on the phone. Telephone discussions tend to me more abbreviated than face-to-face encounters. This factor makes it more difficult for the participants to create the type of psychological commitment to settlement they may generate through in-person conversations. People who cannot meet in person but who would like to have more personal interactions should not hesitate to take advantage of video-conferencing.[1]

Many lawyers believe that telephone discussions are less revealing than face-to-face talks, because they do not involve visual interactions. They think that opposing attorneys cannot perceive nonverbal signals during these interactions. Some psychologists have suggested to me that many individuals are more adept at reading nonverbal messages during telephone exchanges than they are during in-person interactions. Support for this thesis comes from blind students who have exhibited an uncanny capacity to read the nonverbal signals being emitted by others they cannot see. This phenomenon is due to the fact that face-to-face interactions involve many simultaneous nonverbal stimuli that may be too numerous to be proficiently discerned and interpreted. When persons talk on the telephone, they are not as likely to be overwhelmed by the various nonverbal clues emanating from the other party. They concentrate on the audible messages they hear to ascertain the content of the verbal messages being conveyed. They are thus more likely to hear verbal leaks emanating

---

[1] *See* GRANDE LUM, THE NEGOTIATION FIELDBOOK 167–68 (2011).

from the speaker than they might during face-to-face discussions. They also hear a number of nonverbal signals contained in the voices of those with whom they are interacting.

Many nonverbal clues are discernible during telephone discussions. Participants are usually listening intently to the voice of the person speaking. They thus hear changes in the pitch, pace, tone, inflection, and volume of the speaker. A pregnant pause may indicate that a particular offer is being seriously considered by a recipient who did not hesitate before she rejected prior proposals. The other party cannot cover up this hesitation by playing with her glasses or looking at her notes as they could during an in-person discussion. A sigh in response to a new proposal may similarly suggest that the recipient is now confident that some agreement will be reached. Voice inflection may be similarly informative. Persons who respond to new offers with perceptibly increased levels of excitement may nonverbally indicate that they are more pleased with this proposal than their verbal response might indicate.

Lawyers who engage in telephone negotiations should listen intently for verbal leaks and nonverbal signals emanating from their opponents. They should also appreciate the ability of their adversaries to discern their own verbal leaks and nonverbal signals. They should thus try to control their verbal messages and their nonverbal signs as carefully as they would during face-to-face encounters.

It is often advantageous to be the caller, rather than the recipient of calls, during telephone interactions. The caller prepares for the exchange by reviewing her notes of prior discussions and determining exactly what to say at the beginning of the present encounter. They may surprise the recipient of the call who does not recall where the parties were when they last spoke a week or two ago. Despite their complete lack of preparation for this interaction, the recipient of the call is likely to participate as if they were fully prepared. They may forget the fact they made the last concession and bid against themselves by making the next position change. They may not recall particular factual, legal, or economic considerations and disclose more than they would have if they had mentally prepared to negotiate.

Individuals who receive unexpected telephone calls from opposing attorneys should assess their preparedness. If they are not fully conversant regarding the pertinent issues, they should not engage in substantive talks. They should indicate that they are currently occupied and will return the other party's call as soon as they are done with the matter they are dealing with. They should take out the relevant client file and review the relevant information and prior call details. They should then call the other person back and simply say that they are returning that individual's call. Their subsequent silence can force the first caller to initiate the substantive discussions.

Most people find it easier to be less polite during telephone exchanges than during face-to-face interactions, and they find it easier to reject proposals made by others. This is due to the relatively impersonal nature of telephone interactions. If telephone negotiators think their use of this communication medium is undermining their negotiations, they should either employ attitudinal bargaining to alter negative opponent behavior or schedule face-to-face discussions that may prove more successful.

Cell phone interactions create even more complex negotiation difficulties. When we call another attorney on a land line, we know that we are reaching her office. She is unlikely to be significantly distracted by what is going on around her or in a location where her conversation is going to be overheard by complete strangers. When we call someone's cell phone number, we have no idea where they are located. They may be at a reception or party with many other people, or they may be at a tavern watching a sporting event. These external distractions could significantly undermine their ability to focus on the serious discussions we hope to conduct with them. When lawyers call other attorneys on their cell phones, they should ask if this is a good time to talk. If the recipients of the call indicate that they are currently occupied, the callers should ask them to return the call when they are alone.

When individuals talk on their cell phones, then tend to talk more loudly than they do on land lines. When I am on a train or at the airport, I often hear lawyers and business persons talking about highly confidential matters. Their voices are so loud that I can hear the names of the parties involved and even the details of the deal they are discussing. Such careless behavior could violate Model Rule 1.6 which requires attorneys to preserve the confidentiality of client information. Persons who wish to conduct cell phone negotiations should be careful to conduct their discussions in areas where they cannot be heard by complete strangers.

II. E-MAIL NEGOTIATIONS

Computers have made it efficient and practical to conduct bargaining interactions electronically. Parties introduce themselves through e-mail exchanges, and send bargaining proposals back and forth as attached electronic files. This is an especially economical way to deal with parties located in other states or in other countries. Before individuals become overly enamored with electronic negotiating, however, some cautionary considerations should be appreciated.

Bargaining involves ***personal interactions***. It is difficult to have good personal interactions conducted entirely in writing. It is so much easier to establish critical rapport through in-person or telephone exchanges during which the parties talk directly to one another. Professors Leigh Thompson and Janice Nadler of Northwestern University have conducted several interesting studies in this regard.[2] They divided students into pairs and instructed them to conduct negotiation exercises entirely through e-mail exchanges. Half of the participants were given a five-minute schmoozing telephone call during which they could discuss their personal lives, their school experiences, and similar topics. They could not talk about their negotiation exercise. When negotiators who got the preliminary schmoozing phone call worked on their exercises through e-mail exchanges, they behaved more cooperatively, reached more agreements, and achieved more efficient arrangements than the participants who had no preliminary phone calls prior to their e-mail interactions.

It is thus important for persons who plan to conduct their negotiations through e-mail exchanges to take a few minutes to telephone each other to get to know one another and establish some rapport. This is especially important with respect to parties who do not have on-going relationships. Once they have taken the time to talk personally, they can begin to exchange electronic proposals. They must also appreciate the fact that when individuals receive written proposals, they tend to read them carefully, and they often read too much or too little into specific terms. They assume that the sender's proposals are self-serving and somewhat manipulative, even when this is not true. They may thus interpret fair proposals as unfair, and respond accordingly. They may quickly escalate the battle and generate a similar response from the offended original sender. To avoid this phenomenon, proposal senders should telephone the proposal recipients several days after their e-mail messages

---

[2] *See* Leigh Thompson & Janice Nadler, *Negotiating Via Information Technology: Theory and Application*, 58 J. SOCIAL ISSUES 109 (2002).

were sent to hear their responses. Ask them if they have any comments or questions. They may not like particular language that is actually innocuous. If they suggest substitute language conveying the same message, a quick substitution of their language for the original terminology can be disarming. It they are truly upset about a particular provision, the parties can directly discuss their disagreement. They may be able to work out an acceptable compromise. Even if they cannot do so, however, by discussing the term directly with one another they diminish the likelihood their disagreement will generate insurmountable obstacles to a final accord.

Another sad fact of electronic communication concerns the ease with which communicators can flame one another with intemperate comments most would be unlikely to convey in person or on the telephone. Someone receives a communication they find offensive, and they immediately draft a nasty response. If the other side responds in kind, a war of words may develop. If someone conducting e-mail exchanges does not like something said by the other side, they can sit at their computer and type a negative reply. This may make them feel better due to the cathartic nature of their actions. When they are finished, however, they should press the *cancel* button instead of the *send* button, and discard the offensive message they have prepared. They can then prepare a more detached and professional response that would be more likely to generate a constructive response from the other party.

One critical risk often ignored by electronic negotiators concerns the possibility they will convey far more information in their electronic files than they intended to convey. As they prepare their proposals, they request input from clients and colleagues. Those persons suggest new language and explain why they are making their suggestions. Once the proposals are reworked and become final, they are sent via e-mail attachments to the opposing side. Depending upon the software used, many of the alternative formulations may be buried in the electronic files as metadata. Even comments from firm attorneys or received electronically from clients may be imbedded in the metadata. Knowledgeable computer experts may be able to "mine" the electronic files for such information and obtain comments and changes the sender did not intend for them to view.

Is it ethical for the recipients of electronic files to mine those files for metadata that will provide them with drafting changes and drafter comments? In 2006, American Bar Association Formal Opinion 06-442 indicated that lawyers have no ethical duty to refrain from mining and using metadata embedded in electronic files received through e-mail or other modes from opposing parties. On the other hand, the Vermont Bar Association [Vt. Bar Assn. Prof. Respon. Sectopm Op. 2009-1], the Maine Bar Association [Me. Bd. of Bar Overseers Prof. Ethics Comm. Op. 196 (10/26/08)]; the New York Bar Association [N.Y. State Ethics Op. 749 (2001)] and the Alabama Bar Association [Ala. State Bar Disc. Comm. Op. 2007-02 (2007)] have indicated that such mining of metadata in electronic files constitutes an improper attempt by the file recipients to obtain privileged information they have no right to see in an effort to obtain an unfair advantage over the other side. The District of Columbia Bar Association [D.C. Legal Ethics Committee Op. 341 (9/07)] recently took an intermediate position, indicating that while lawyers should not review metadata embedded in electronic files sent to them by other attorneys when they have actual knowledge that the metadata was sent inadvertently, they may mine the metadata when it is not clear that the hidden electronic information was not inadvertently included.

The Minnesota Bar Association [Minn. Lawyers Prof. Respon. Bd. Op. 22 (3/26/10)], the New York Bar Association [N.Y. State Ethics Op. 782 (2004)], and the

Alabama Bar Association [Ala. State Bar Disc. Comm. Op. 2007-2 (2007)] have indicated that lawyers have an obligation under the rules governing client confidentiality to use "reasonable care" when transmitting electronic documents to prevent the inadvertent disclosure of metadata containing client confidences. It thus behooves lawyers and others to employ means designed to prevent the unintended disclosure of confidential information when they convey electronic files. To avoid the disclosure of such information contained in metadata, lawyers should send PDF files of the requisite documents, or they should open new files and then insert the old files into the new files. The files being inserted into the newly created files will no longer contain the metadata that was included in the original files. Attorneys can also use one of several file scrubbing software programs that will eliminate the metadata from files before they are sent to others.

TELEPHONE/E-MAIL NEGOTIATION EXERCISES

It can be helpful for readers to work on a negotiation exercise that must be conducted entirely by phone. They usually find this fairly easy to do. The major difference between this and face-to-face interactions concerns the greater number of phone exchanges compared with in-person talks. When they interact on a face-to-face basis, they often achieve agreements in one or two sessions. When telephone interactions are involved, they may exchange ten or more phone calls, since they rarely conduct the type of detailed negotiations over the phone they conduct during in-person exchanges. On the other hand, since they are usually well prepared for these telephone negotiations due to the fact they take place during a relatively short time frame, the results they achieve do not differ from what they would have achieved during face-to-face negotiations.

It can also be informative for persons to engage in an exercise that must be negotiated entirely through e-mail exchanges. Participants may not use any other means of communication. Most find these interactions to be far less personal than face-to-face negotiations, and these encounters usually generate a greater number of nonsettlements than in-person interactions. This reflects the fact it is easier to behave more competitively and less pleasantly during e-mail exchanges. It is also easier to reject final opponent offers due to the lack of any personal connection between the participants. A few individuals suggest a liking for e-mail negotiations, due to the fact they are not required to think as quickly as they are during face-to-face interactions. I consider this a negative factor, since proficient negotiators should be able to react effectively to opposing party disclosures and proposals.

Readers should pair off and work on a negotiation exercise that must be conducted entirely through e-mail exchanges. Half of the participants could be allowed five minutes of schmoozing — either by telephone or in person. They may not discuss the exercise in any way during this period. After they have completed the schmoozing period, they must negotiate the exercise via e-mail exchanges.

SELF-ASSESSMENT

SELF-ASSESSMENT

Did the negotiators find it easier or more difficult to conduct their interactions entirely through e-mail? Did they like or dislike the depersonalized nature of such interactions? Did they like or dislike the fact they did not engage in the simultaneous verbal and nonverbal exchanges associated with in-person negotiations?

If half of the negotiating pairs were given five minute schmoozing opportunities prior to their bargaining interactions, did these pairs achieve more efficient terms than the pairs that were not provided with this opportunity?

Do you think it is ethical or unethical for negotiators to mine the metadata in files sent by e-mail to see all of the changes that have been made in those files? Do you think most attorneys are even aware of the metadata contained in their electronic files? Do you think that law students who send resumes and writing samples electronically to law firms in Word or WordPerfect formats realize that the attorneys viewing those files can see every change they have made in them?

Chapter 15
INTERNATIONAL BUSINESS NEGOTIATIONS

In his thoughtful book *The World is Flat* (2005), Thomas Friedman discussed the degree to which most major business enterprises have become transnational in scope. Their headquarters are located in one country, they obtain raw materials from several different nations, they operate labor intensive manufacturing facilities in a number of emerging countries, and they do business in even more countries. Most of these multinational enterprises are no longer ethnocentric focusing on their home nations. They have become geocentric entities that seek to maximize shareholder returns through operations in different nations. No single country can effectively regulate their global activities, and no international organization does so either.

As national economies have become inextricably intertwined with the economies of other countries, corporate leaders have had to become more proficient international business negotiators. Creation of the North American Free Trade Agreement by the United States, Mexico, and Canada has generated many business arrangements among business firms from all three countries. As the European Union has expanded from Western European nations to a number of Eastern European countries, United States executives have had to negotiate with business officials in these diverse nations. Many corporations have entered into business deals with local firms in African and Asian nations.

A substantial number of products sold in the United States have been manufactured in China and other lower-cost nations. Many computer firms employ programers who reside in India, and many 800 number services are provided by persons living in Bangalore. Wal-Mart requires many of its largest suppliers of goods to operate manufacturing facilities in China.[1] General Motors, Ford, and Chrysler have joint ventures with firms around the world, and Toyota and Nissan operate major manufacturing facilities within the United States. All of these business arrangements have been generated through transnational negotiations.

International business negotiations are complicated by various factors. The substantial distances between the United States and the other countries make it necessary for the negotiators to travel long distances. Executives who travel significant distances may experience jet lag and may fear that their presence in the other firm's territory may suggest over-eagerness on their firm's behalf. They may feel pressure to consummate final deals before they return home. To avoid these problems, they should fly to the other countries a day or two before they are scheduled to begin their negotiations, and they should be flexible regarding the dates they plan to return home. If they are unable to achieve final agreements during these discussions, they should not hesitate to schedule future talks.

Most persons do not feel comfortable negotiating with others in foreign countries. They miss their own homes, and have to adjust to unfamiliar foods. They have to adjust to different cultures, and languages most do not speak fluently — if at all. They are usually obliged to accept hospitality from their opponent-hosts, and this may induce them to make concessions they might not otherwise make.

---

[1] *See generally* CHARLES FISHMAN, THE WAL-MART EFFECT (2006).

Americans tend to be impatient negotiators. They travel to foreign nations, meet their opposing executives, and ask them what they want to obtain. Due to the cultural differences and the lack of familiarity between the different participants, it is especially important for such negotiators to have an extended Preliminary Stage. They need to get to know the other side and to establish some rapport with those persons. They should read up on the other side's culture, and try to learn something from their hosts about their culture. Most people are proud of their national heritages, and they like to share it with outsiders. On the other hand, when visitors show a disdain for their cultures, they take it personally.

Impatient negotiators should try not to place themselves in positions in which they feel the need to achieve accords before they return home. In some cases, they should initially travel to other countries simply to get to know the other side. They should avoid significant substantive discussions during these preliminary talks. Once they establish sound working relationships, they can get together again to move toward definitive agreements.

Another critical factor pertaining to international business negotiations concerns the fact that different legal norms may be involved. Each negotiator has to comply with the laws of their own country, and they must appreciate the impact of the opposing side's laws on both participants. This is why transnational business negotiators usually employ lawyers from both their own country and from the nation of the executives with whom they are interacting. They must be aware of both the formal legal principles, and the informal doctrines and practices that may modify the literal statutes and regulations. Will government agencies be directly involved in these negotiations, or indirectly involved? What forms of government approval will be required before negotiated deals can be effectuated? What is the most efficient way to move proposed arrangements through the requisite governmental channels?

When Americans interact with other Americans, they tend to assume common cultural norms, even when the participants are from different areas of the country. Verbal expressions and nonverbal signals have common meanings, and the participants tend to share common values. On the other hand, when Americans interact with persons from foreign cultures, they must recognize the influence of cultural differences.[2] Positive and negative stereotyping may affect their bargaining interactions. Particular traits may be attributed to individual participants based upon their nationalities that bear no relationship to reality.

Punctuality is more important to typical Americans than it is to people from many other cultures. If an American arrived more than five or ten minutes late for a scheduled meeting, she would be considered rude, while a thirty or forty-five minute delay would be acceptable in most Latin American or Middle-Eastern countries. Americans tend to separate business and social talks, while persons from other countries often conduct business discussions during social functions.

Spatial distances may vary widely depending upon the culture involved. In the United States, most persons who do not know each other quite well tend to remain eighteen to twenty-four inches apart, particularly during business discussions. In other cultures, however, such as Middle-Eastern countries, an eight to twelve inch separation may be considered acceptable. Americans feel uncomfortable with such close spatial distances, and they tend to move away from such close situations. This may cause them to be perceived by others as cold or disinterested.

---

[2] See generally JEANNE M. BRETT, NEGOTIATING GLOBALLY (2001); JESWALD W. SALACUS, THE GLOBAL NEGOTIATOR (2003).

The United States is a highly individualistic culture, with individual independence being valued more than group cohesiveness. Americans tend to reward individuals who exhibit autonomous behavior designed to advance their own interests. They value personal privacy and freedom. They work to advance employer interests more to demonstrate their own capabilities than to contribute to the overall success of the collective business. Other cultures have a collectivistic orientation. Persons in such cultures are defined more by their family and business ties than by their individual accomplishments. They are expected to work with others to advance group interests. Managers consult their colleagues before they make important decisions, with final determinations being made through a consensus process. People in collectivist cultures often dislike bargaining interactions, because they do not like conflict and dislike the loss of face often associated with the give-and-take of the negotiation process.

Most American negotiators do not hesitate to employ overt power displays, while in other cultures (*e.g.*, Japan) such open displays of power would be considered unacceptable. Americans also tend to feel comfortable using aggressive tactics, while persons from other cultures may not. In all bargaining interactions — especially those from different cultures — Americans should remember that negotiators can be forceful without being pushy.

Persons from disparate socio-economic backgrounds often find it hard to appreciate each other's perspectives with respect to delayed gratification. Individuals from wealthy countries tend to accept the notion of delayed gratification, based upon the financial success of their ancestors, but persons from poor countries are less inclined to postpone present gratification for the hope of achieving greater future returns. When United States negotiators interact with individuals from emerging nations, they may have to initially emphasize the short-term benefits of their prospective deals over the long-term possibilities if they hope to achieve agreements.

Before Americans interact with negotiators from different countries, they should read about the cultural backgrounds of the foreign nations involved.[3] Foreigners frequently complain about the insensitivity of Americans to such factors. Americans who demonstrate an understanding of and respect for the historical developments and cultures of other countries are likely to find greater acceptance by people from those nations.

When international business deals are being negotiated, currency issues may become significant. Are monetary terms to be defined in U.S. dollars or the currency of the other countries involved? Which party is willing to assume the risk of currency fluctuation? In some cases, the parties may agree to specify monetary items in terms of an more expansive currency such as the Euro.

Different employment philosophies may influence business deals. In the United States, the employment-as-will policy allows private sector employers to terminate employees at almost any time for almost any reason. In other countries, however, wrongful termination policies may restrict such practices. Firms wishing to terminate individuals without just cause may be required to provide the affected persons with severance payments.

Most Americans view business deals as legally enforceable arrangements that should be defined with specificity in the operative contracts. Corporate leaders from

---

[3] For discussions of the general cultures of many countries, see OLEGARIO LLAMAZARES, HOW TO NEGOTIATE SUCCESSFULLY IN 50 COUNTRIES (2008); TERRI MORRISON & WAYNE CONAWAY, KISS, BOW, OR SHAKE HANDS (2006).

other countries (*e.g.*, Asian nations) tend to be more relationship oriented. They base their business ties more on mutual trust than on contractual obligations. As a result they take longer during the Preliminary Stage to establish good working relationships, and they tend to negotiate contracts containing more general terms. When specific questions arise with respect to their arrangement, they plan to work them out through joint discussions. They are offended by negotiators who try to define every contract term with precise language, believing that such behavior evidences a lack of respect for their integrity.

When international business deals are negotiated, language issues may arise. Although English has become a truly international language, representatives from other countries may not like to conduct negotiations in English preferring to use their own native language. If this is true, each party should have a skilled interpreter who appreciates the subtleties of each language involved. Even when the talks are conducted in English, misunderstandings may develop. Foreigners may interpret verbal statements and nonverbal signals differently from their American counterparts. American representatives should speak clearly and more deliberately, and they should avoid the use of slang expressions that may not be understood by persons who have never lived in the United States.

The United States is a *low context* culture. We tend to say what we mean, allowing others to know exactly what we intend to convey. In *high context* cultures (*e.g.*, Japan), however, people convey messages more indirectly. This is especially true when they have to provide someone with negative information. In these situations, it is important to evaluate the surrounding circumstances to understand the true meaning being communicated. For example, if an American negotiator wishes to reject an opponent's proposal, she is likely to say "no." In Japan, the speaker would be unlikely to be so direct to avoid a loss of "face" by the other party. He would be likely to say "we will try" — which means "perhaps" — or "that would be difficult" — which means "no."

Language can become a critical issue when the parties have to designate the official language for their agreement. Most negotiators prefer to have the official language the language of their own country. To avoid overt conflicts over this issue, the parties may designate the languages of their respective nations as joint official languages, or they may select a neutral third language.

Most corporations are hesitant to expose themselves to the laws of other countries or to the jurisdiction of foreign courts. As a result, they may simply provide that the legal doctrines generally applied to international business transactions will govern their relationship. They may then select a private dispute resolution mechanism that will be used to handle any disagreements that may arise during their contract. If inter-party negotiations are unable to resolve such conflicts, parties usually employ the assistance of a mediator. If such a neutral facilitator is unable to get the parties to a mutual accord, they are likely to use binding arbitration. They may use a single neutral arbitrator, three neutral arbitrators, or a tripartite arbitration system under which each party selects a preferred arbitrator and they jointly select a neutral arbitral chair.

NEGOTIATION EXERCISE

The following international negotiation exercise is designed to introduce readers to this important and interesting area. I have deliberately refrained from assigning specific points to each issue, to make the exercise more like what lawyers encounter in the real world. Participants should be divided into pairs with half designated Mu

Electronics representatives and half Eastern Electric representatives. The persons who represent Mu Electronics should try to conduct themselves the way in which they think Chinese negotiators would behave, while the Eastern Electric representatives should try to behave like American lawyers.

GENERAL INFORMATION — CHINESE JOINT VENTURE

The Eastern Electric Light Company, a Delaware Corporation, has been manufacturing light bulbs and small electrical appliances since 1923. Eastern Electric has been doing well financially in recent years, with gross revenues for the last fiscal year of $350,000,000. It has been thinking of entering the expanding market in the People's Republic of China ("China"), but is unwilling to enter that market alone. It would thus like to develop a joint venture with a Chinese firm. It was recently contacted by Mu Electronics, a three-year old limited liability company headquartered in Beijing. Mu Electronics also manufactures light bulbs and small electrical appliances, but its factory consists of an antiquated facility that was formerly owned and operated by the Chinese Government. Despite the inefficiencies associated with such an old plant, Mu Electronics has been doing remarkably well for a newly-formed company. Last year, it had gross sales of $10,000,000. The Mu Electronics managers think that they could generate much greater revenues if they could obtain an infusion of foreign funds, modernize their existing facility, and develop a national sales campaign.

Representatives of Eastern Electric and Mu Electronics are endeavoring to negotiate the terms of a mutually acceptable joint venture. They must agree upon the financial support to be provided by Eastern Electric, the percentage of Mu Electronics stock Eastern Electric is to acquire, the collateral Eastern Electric is to be given in case the joint venture fails or the Chinese Government decides to nationalize Mu Electronics, the official language to be used in the official joint venture documents, the applicable law to govern future contractual disputes, the dispute resolution procedures to be used to resolve any such controversies, and any other matters the representatives consider important.

CONFIDENTIAL INFORMATION — EASTERN ELECTRIC

CONFIDENTIAL INFORMATION — EASTERN ELECTRIC

Mu Electronics provides Eastern Electric with the exact target of opportunity it has been seeking. It is a new, but already successful, firm with outstanding managers and a well-trained labor force. Eastern Electric believes that the infusion of new capital should enable a modernized Mu Electronics to greatly expand its currently limited production. You have thus been instructed to reach a joint venture agreement with Mu Electronics if at all possible.

Eastern Electric realizes that Mu Electronics will require an initial infusion of approximately $25,000,000 to modernize the production facility and will probably require about $10,000,000 per year for the next few years to develop a national sales campaign. If these goals are achieved, it is believed that Mu Electronics could increase its current $10,000,000 gross revenues to the $50-75 million range. You have thus been authorized to agree to the $25,000,000 initial outlay and to $10,000,000 per year thereafter for the following four years. You should be extremely reluctant to promise financial support above these figures over the first five years, and should refuse to make any definitive commitments beyond the first five years of this joint venture — unless absolutely necessary. If the projected joint venture revenue figures are not met during this time frame, Eastern Electric would be hesitant to contribute further financial support.

Chinese businesses do not like to have foreign firms hold a majority ownership in Chinese corporations. If possible, Eastern Electric would like to obtain a fifty percent share that would give it the same power possessed by Mu Electronics. It would also like to have the name of the joint venture firm changed to "Mu-Eastern Electronics." If you are unable to achieve a 50-50 share division, you must at least obtain a promise that Eastern Electric will be given one-quarter of Mu Electronics shares by the end of the first year and one-third of Mu Electronics shares by the end of the initial five year period. Eastern Electric would also like to be guaranteed the right to immediately name one-quarter of the Mu Electronics Corporate Board members and to name one-third of the Board by the end of the initial five-year period. It would also like to be able to immediately name one Executive Vice President of Mu Electronics and to be able to name a second Executive Vice President within the next five years. (Mu Electronics currently has seven Executive Vice Presidents.)

Eastern Electric would like to be guaranteed fifty percent of Mu Electronics profits. If it is unable to achieve this profit division, it would like to be promised a profit split in proportion to its share of Mu Electronics shares.

Eastern Electric is concerned about the uncertain fate of the free market system in China in the coming years. If Communist hard-liners regain control, they may outlaw private firms and nationalize existing businesses. To protect Eastern Electric interests, you have been instructed to seek a provision giving Eastern Electric a secured interest in the building, equipment, and real property of Mu Electronics. It would also like to obtain the right to petition the Chinese Government for just compensation for any Mu Electronics property that is nationalized.

You must agree with Mu Electronics whether English, Chinese, or some third language is to be the official contract language. Although you would prefer English to govern, you recognize that Mu Electronics will probably reject this option. If you are unable to obtain English as the official language, you would prefer to have English and Chinese texts govern jointly. If compelled, however, you may reluctantly agree to Chinese as the official language.

You must also agree upon the legal doctrines to govern the interpretation and application of your joint venture agreement. Eastern Electric would prefer to have United States law and the Delaware Corporate Code govern and is unalterably opposed to reliance on Chinese law due to the uncertainty surrounding the evolving Chinese law regulating private business arrangements. If you cannot obtain an agreement to apply United States law, you would like to get Mu Electronics to agree to the application of European Union doctrines. If this proposal is unacceptable to Mu Electronics, you would then prefer language merely stating that the terms of your joint venture agreement will be interpreted according to business doctrines that are generally applied by the international community when resolving transnational business controversies.

Since Mu Electronics is unlikely to submit itself to jurisdiction of United States courts and Eastern Electric is unwilling to subject itself to the jurisdiction of Chinese judicial tribunals, you must agree upon a mutually acceptable procedure to resolve contractual disputes that may arise. You would like to specify that the Presidents, or their designates, of Eastern Electric and Mu Electronics will initially endeavor to negotiate an acceptable resolution of any disagreement regarding the interpretation and application of the joint venture agreement. In case these efforts are not successful, you would like to specify a list of three or four respected international conciliators who would be used on a rotating basis to mediate any disputes. In case conciliation efforts are unsuccessful, you would like to use binding arbitration procedures to resolve the matter. You would prefer a tripartite system under which Eastern Electric and Mu Electronics representatives would each appoint their own arbitrator, with these two individuals attempting to agree upon a third neutral arbitrator. Should the designated arbitrators be unable to agree upon the neutral arbitrator, you would like to require the parties to follow the appointment procedure used by the International Chamber of Commerce. You would like a requirement that all designated mediators and arbitrators be fluent in both English and Chinese

CONFIDENTIAL INFORMATION — MU ELECTRONICS

CONFIDENTIAL INFORMATION — MU ELECTRONICS

Mu Electronics desperately requires external financial support. Although it has experienced great financial success during its first three years of existence, it needs millions of dollars to modernize its antiquated manufacturing facility. With new financial support, Mu Electronics could probably expand sales throughout China and increase gross annual revenues from the current $10,000,000 to the $75,000,000 or even $100,000,000 range. Since no other firms have expressed an interest in a joint venture with Mu Electronics, it is imperative that you achieve a mutually acceptable arrangement with Eastern Electric.

Mu Electronics has estimated that it will take an initial investment of at least $15,000,000 to modernize its existing production plant. To provide some leeway, you have been instructed to seek as much over this $15,000,000 initial investment figure as possible. After the first year plant changes, Mu Electronics believes that it will take a minimum of $5,000,000 per year to generate a national sales campaign. If you could obtain commitments in excess of this $5,000,000 per year figure, this would greatly enhance the future prospects of Mu Electronics. You would like to obtain such an annual commitment for nine years following the plant modernization year, but would be willing to accept a shorter commitment if necessary. If you cannot get a full nine-year commitment, you would like to obtain a general promise that Eastern Electric will endeavor to continue this annual support so long as annual revenues are increasing.

Chinese corporations generally do not agree to majority ownership of Chinese firms by foreign interests. Mu Electronics is thus unwilling to allow Eastern Electric to hold over fifty percent of the Mu Electronics shares. While Eastern Electric may seek a fifty percent share interest, this would be wholly unacceptable to Mu Electronics which insists on maintaining majority interest. You may grant a thirty percent interest to Eastern Electric as soon as the joint venture is agreed upon. Assuming Eastern Electric continues to provide annual financial support of at least $5,000,000, you may also agree to grant that firm a forty percent interest by the end of the fifth year of the new relationship. You should only exceed forty percent with great reluctance, and you may not grant more than a forty-five percent share under any circumstances. Since your firm is named after Mr. Mu, the founder of the business, you would like to retain the Mu Electronics name in future years.

It is likely that Eastern Electric will demand the right to select several members of the Mu Electronics Board of Directors. Since that firm will hold at least a quarter of Mu Electronics shares, you would be perfectly willing to let Eastern Electric name one-quarter of the Corporate Board members. By the end of the initial five-year period, you may even permit Eastern Electric to name up to forty percent of the Corporate Board. You may not, however, allow that company to name over forty percent.

Mu Electronics currently has seven Executive Vice Presidents. It assumes that Eastern Electric will insist on the right to name one, two, or possibly even three Executive Vice Presidents to protect its economic interest in Mu Electronics. Since such a request is common in joint ventures, you are authorized to agree to Eastern Electric control over one or even two Executive Vice Presidencies. Since Mu Electronics has been planning to expand the number of Executive Vice Presidents from seven to ten, you may agree to let Eastern Electric name three Executive Vice Presidents, so long as this is only done after the total number is expanded to ten.

You anticipate that Eastern Electric will demand the right to half of the profits generated by Mu Electronics following the joint venture. Your firm considers this an excessive figure, and will not accept any deal that gives Eastern Electric more than forty percent of Mu Electronics profits. You have been authorized to give Eastern Electric a profit share equal to the percent of Mu Electronics shares held by that firm — *i.e.*, up to thirty percent at the outset and up to forty percent by the end of the initial five year period.

Mu Electronics recognizes that Eastern Electric is concerned about the uncertain future of the free market in China and fears nationalization of private firms if Communist hard-liners regain control. You suspect that Eastern Electric will ask for a secured interest in the building, equipment, and real property of Mu Electronics. You are perfectly willing to agree to such a provision.

Mu Electronics would like to have the Chinese draft of the joint venture contract constitute the official draft and will not permit the English draft to govern. If you are unable to obtain an agreement specifying that the Chinese draft is controlling, you would be willing to allow the English and Chinese texts to govern jointly.

The parties must agree upon the legal doctrines that will govern the interpretation and application of their joint venture agreement. Mu Electronics would like to have Chinese law apply, but realizes the hesitancy of foreign firms to agree to such an arrangement due to the evolving nature of Chinese private venture legal doctrines. Mu Electronics is unalterably opposed to the application of United States law to contractual matters, because it fears the law will favor U.S. companies. You have been authorized to agree to the application of European Union doctrines, and if this is unacceptable, to a provision merely stating that the terms of the joint venture agreement will be interpreted according to business doctrines generally applicable by the international community when resolving transactional business disputes.

Mu Electronics is unwilling to submit itself to jurisdiction of United States courts and assumes that Eastern Electric would be unwilling to submit to Chinese judicial jurisdiction. As a result, the parties must agree upon a mutually acceptable dispute resolution procedure. You are willing to allow the assistance of internationally respected mediators, and would even be willing to submit unresolved controversies to an international arbitral panel. You are flexible regarding the exact arbitrator selection procedures, so long as the procedures would guarantee the selection of qualified neutrals who are fluent in Chinese.

SELF-ASSESSMENT

SELF-ASSESSMENT

Were participants who represented Mu Electronics able to place themselves in the shoes of their corporate client? During the negotiations, did they behave primarily like American attorneys representing a foreign client or did they try to act as if they were Chinese lawyers? Were they very direct in their discussions, as are most American negotiators, or more indirect, as are most Chinese negotiators? Did they behave more individualistically, as do most Americans, or in more of a group oriented manner, as do most Chinese?

In most international business negotiations of this kind, both corporations would be likely to employ American and Chinese attorneys to participate in the negotiations. It thus becomes imperative for the two groups of attorneys on each side to work together during the Preparation Stage to put together a set of common objectives and to develop a unified negotiation strategy.

Participants can compare their results with the comparison grid provided on the following page, even though specific points were not assigned to the different issues to be negotiated. Did they do a good job of achieving the objectives of their own clients and of generating agreements that maximized the joint returns achieved by both sides?

	EASTERN ELECTR.	**MU ELECTR.**
INIT. INVEST. PER YEAR	Up to $25 Mill. $10 Mill. per to 4 Yrs avoid longer commit.	At least $15 Mill. $5 Mill./Yr. for 9 Yrs shorter term accept.
CORP. CONTROL	Goal: 50/50 Share Split At least 25% by 1st Yr. 1/3 by end of 5th Yr. "Mu-Eastern Electr." If possib. Name 1/4 corp. bd. now 1/3 bd. by end of 5th yr.	Initl. 30% Share Split 40% by end of 5th Yr. max. of 45% Keep Mu Name if Possib Mu-Eastern if need be Name 1/4 corp. bd. now Up to 40% by 5th yr.
EXEC. VPs NOW	Name 1 exec VP now name another by Yr. 5	Name 1 or 2 VP now up to 3 when 10 VPs.
PROFITS	50% if possib. at least % of shares held	% of shares held 30% now 40–45% by 5th Yr.
SECURED INT.	Bldg., equip. & real prop.	Bldg., equip. & real
OFFICIAL DRAFT	1) English 2) Jt. Eng.-Chin. 3) Chinese if necessary	1) Chinese 2) Jt. Eng.-Chinese
LEGAL RULES	1) U.S./Del. Corp. Code 2) EU doctrines 3) Bus. Doctrines gen. applied in intl. bus community	1) Cchinese rules 2) EU doctrines 3) Bus. Doctrines gen. applied in intl. bus. Community
DISP. RES. PROC.	1) firm Pres. To discuss 2) list of 3–4 intl. meds. 3) binding tri-partite arb. If neutral arb. not agreed to apt. By intl. Chamb. of Commerce All neutrals fluent in Eng. & Chinese	1) asst. of intl. meds. 2) Iintl. arb. Panel flexible re arb. selection rules Neutrals fluent in Chinese

Chapter 16
HUMAN RIGHTS NEGOTIATIONS

As many large corporations have decided to relocate production facilities to emerging nations where they can obtain the benefit of low-cost labor, various human rights violations have been discerned. In some countries, local plants employ child labor at unconscionably low wages, while in others slave labor is utilized. Basic health and safety standards are ignored, as production firms strive to maintain rock-bottom employment costs. These abuses have been especially prevalent with respect to textile and clothing manufacturers. A number of well-known brand name companies have been embarrassed by media disclosures of the negative working conditions in which their goods are manufactured.

The International Labor Organization (ILO) has established conventions designed to ensure the governmental and corporate acceptance of basic health and safety standards, and to preclude the use of child and slave labor. Despite the adoption of these conventions by most industrial nations, many countries continue to allow factories to operate that do not meet these fundamental standards. The ILO possesses minimal enforcement authority, thus it relies primarily upon individual nations to prevent such abusive employment conditions.

Human Rights Watch has similarly worked to eliminate production facilities in situations involving wholly inadequate employment conditions. Parties failing to maintain minimal standards are placed on the Human Rights Watch list of violators, with the resulting negative publicity acting as a strong incentive for corporations and countries to maintain acceptable conditions.

Other organizations have also been created to monitor the employment conditions used by multinational enterprises to manufacture goods in emerging nations. They use media exposure and public pressure to embarrass firms that fail to ensure the presence of minimal terms of employment. Many major corporations have decided that it can work to their economic advantage to avoid negative publicity concerning child and slave labor and unsafe and unhealthy employment environments. A number even advertise their compliance with ILO and Human Rights Watch standards to encourage customers to purchase their products.

NEGOTIATION EXERCISE

The following exercise involves efforts by a newly formed group, the Human Rights Committee, to negotiate an agreement with Ace Sporting Goods that will preclude the manufacture of Ace products in factories that fail to satisfy minimum standards. Readers should be divided into groups of one or two members and designated Ace Sporting Goods or Human Rights Committee representatives. Negotiators on each side should carefully think about the objectives their own side hopes to achieve — and the objectives they think would be of the greatest significance to the other side.

GENERAL INFORMATION — ACE SPORTING GOODS & HUMAN RIGHTS COMMITTEE

Ace Sporting Goods is a multinational firm that manufactures and sells sportswear and sports equipment. Total sales during the past year exceeded $3 billion. It has production facilities in a number of emerging nations, many of which have not yet been scrutinized by the well-known Human Rights Watch organization. Recent news stories have reported that some of the Ace facilities employ child labor, unpaid slave labor, and grossly underpaid general labor in unhealthy and unsafe work environments. The Human Rights Committee is a one year old nonprofit organization dedicated to the advance of human rights in general and humane working conditions in particular.

As a result of the recent news stories, a number of public interest groups have demanded a total boycott of Ace products. Students at different colleges have demanded that their respective sports teams refrain from any dealings with Ace.

Last week, the CEO of Ace Sporting Goods contacted the Human Rights Committee to discuss a possible agreement under which Ace would promise to end the unconscionable practices at its foreign production plants in exchange for a Human Rights Committee acknowledgment of appropriate employment practices.

CONFIDENTIAL INFORMATION — HUMAN RIGHTS COMMITTEE

CONFIDENTIAL INFORMATION — HUMAN RIGHTS COMMITTEE

Since the formation of your Committee one year ago, your group has been looking for a way to have a significant public impact that would enhance its image and advance its fund-raising efforts. The Managing Committee is eager to achieve a beneficial agreement with Ace Sporting Goods that would be of great assistance in this regard. It is thus imperative that you take advantage of this unique opportunity. If you fail to do so and are unable to reach any agreement with Ace, you will be placed at the ***bottom*** of all Human Rights Committee groups.

It is imperative that you get Ace to agree to the elimination of child labor and slave labor at any facilities manufacturing Ace products. Score ***plus 30 points*** for an Ace agreement to eliminate ***child labor***. Score ***plus 30 points*** for an Ace agreement to eliminate ***slave labor***. Although Ace currently has no production facilities in countries on the Human Rights Watch list of basic human rights violators, you would like Ace to agree that it will not operate any plants in countries on that list. Score ***plus 75 points*** for such an Ace commitment.

Your Committee is also concerned about the unhealthful and unsafe conditions under which Ace products are manufactured. Score ***plus 50 points*** for an agreement requiring Ace to maintain healthful and safe work environments that conform to International Labor Organization standards.

At many of the Ace production facilities, even the general workers are paid less than the average workers employed in the countries in which those plants operate. For a multi-billion dollar sporting goods firm, this is intolerable. Score ***plus 25 points*** if Ace agrees to provide wages ***equal*** to the ***average wages*** earned by individuals employed in the countries in which those plants operate. Score ***plus 50 points*** if Ace agrees to provide wages equal to ***125%*** the average wages in those countries. Score ***plus 75 points*** if Ace agrees to provide wages equal to ***150%*** of the average wages in those countries. Score ***plus 100 points*** if Ace agrees to provide wages equal to ***175%*** of the average wages in those countries. Score ***plus 125 points*** if Ace agrees to provide wages equal to ***200%*** of the average wages in those countries. Score ***plus 150 points*** if Ace agrees to provide wages equal to ***225%*** of the average wages in those countries. Score ***plus 200 points*** if Ace agrees to provide wages equal to ***over 225%*** of the average wages in those countries.

You recognize that Ace may readily agree to improved employment conditions and not ensure their implementation. You thus wish to establish an appropriate monitoring system and, if possible, impose liquidated damages for violations. Score ***plus 50 points*** if Ace agrees to allow a Human Rights Committee group monitor its compliance with the terms agreed upon. Score ***plus 50 points*** if Ace agrees to pay the Human Rights Committee liquidated damages of ***$50,000*** for each violation. Score ***plus 75 points*** if Ace agrees to pay ***$75,000*** for each violation. Score ***plus 100 points*** if Ace agrees to pay ***$100,000*** for each violation. Score ***plus 125 points*** if Ace agrees to pay ***$125,000*** for each violation. Score ***plus 150 points*** if Ace agrees to pay ***$150,000*** for each violation. Score ***plus 200 points*** if Ace agrees to pay ***over $150,000*** for each violation.

The Human Rights Committee would like to generate some beneficial publicity for itself for any agreement reached with Ace. Score ***plus 50 points*** if Ace agrees to allow the Human Rights Committee to issue a press release detailing the terms of any agreement achieved with Ace. Score a ***separate 50 points*** if the Ace CEO agrees to participate in a joint press conference with Human Rights Committee officials announcing the terms agreed upon.

CONFIDENTIAL INFORMATION — ACE SPORTING GOODS

CONFIDENTIAL INFORMATION — ACE SPORTING GOODS

Your firm is painfully aware of the negative impact generated by the recent media stories discussing the substandard conditions at Ace factories in emerging nations. As a result of consumer boycotts, Ace revenues have declined by 18 percent over the past six months. Your CEO had decided that it would be highly beneficial for Ace to agree with the Human Rights Committee to maintain humane working conditions at its foreign production facilities. The increased labor costs would not be that great, and could be offset by modest product price increases. Ace also believes that the enhanced public image it could develop through such an agreement would generate increased product sales. As a result, should you fail to achieve an agreement with the Human Rights Committee, you will have failed your client and be placed at the **bottom** of all Human Rights Committee groups.

Even top Ace officials were surprised and embarrassed to discover the use of child labor and slave labor at some of the Ace manufacturing facilities. They would like to eliminate such practices immediately. Score **plus 25 points** for an agreement to eliminate all **child labor** at Ace facilities. Score **plus 25 points** for an agreement to eliminate all **slave labor** at such facilities. You realize that the Human Rights Committee may also seek an agreement that would preclude Ace from operating any production facility in any country on the Human Rights Watch list of nations with basic human rights violations. Ace currently has no plants in such countries and has no plans to open any in such locations. Since Ace officials believe that it would make the company look public minded to agree not to operate any plants in countries on the Human Rights Watch list, score **plus 50 points** for such an Ace commitment.

Ace officials also recognize the need to ensure that their goods are manufactured in healthy and safe environments. Score **plus 25 points** for an agreement to maintain work environments at all production facilities that conform to the health and safety standards set forth in International Labor Organization pronouncements.

At many of the Ace production facilities, even the general workers are paid less than the average workers employed in the countries in which the plants operate. Ace is perfectly willing to agree to provide workers with wages equal to the **average wages** earned by persons in the countries in which those plants operate and you lose **no points** for such a commitment. Ace would not like to see labor increase too much, however, to enable it to maintain competitive prices for its products.

Score **minus 50 points** if you agree to increase wages to **125%** of the average wages in those countries. Score **minus 75 points** if you agree to increase wages to **150%** of the average wages in those countries. Score **minus 100 points** if you agree to increase wages to **175%** of the average wages in those countries. Score **minus 150 points** if you agree to increase wages to **200%** of the average wages in those countries. Score **minus 200 points** if you agree to increase wages to **225%** of the average wages in those countries. Score **minus 500 points** if you agree to increase wages to **over 225%** of the average wages in those countries.

Ace realizes that the Human Rights Committee will seek to have a monitoring system created to ensure Ace compliance with the new employment terms agreed upon. Ace would like to have its own Human Resources Department perform this function. Score **plus 25 points** for an agreement allowing Ace to be the **sole monitor** of its compliance. Score **minus 25 points** if you agree to allow a Human Rights Committee group monitor Ace compliance.

It is common for human rights groups to impose liquidated damages for violations of agreements mandating minimum employment conditions. Score **minus 50 points** if

Ace agrees to pay *$50,000* for each violation. Score *minus 75 points* if Ace agrees to pay *$75,000* for each violation. Score *minus 100 points* if Ace agrees to pay *$100,000* for each violation. Score *minus 150 points* if Ace agrees to pay *$125,000* for each violation. Score *minus 200* if Ace agrees to pay *$150,000* for each violation. Score *minus 500 points* if Ace agrees to pay *over $150,000* for each violation.

The Ace CEO hopes to generate highly beneficial publicity from any agreement reached with the Human Rights Committee. Score *plus 50 points* if the Human Rights Committee agrees to allow Ace to issue a press release detailing the terms agreed upon. Score *plus 50 points* if Human Rights Committee representatives agree to participate in a joint press conference with Ace officials explaining the terms agreed upon.

SELF-ASSESSMENT

SELF-ASSESSMENT

Did the negotiators on each side try to place themselves in the shoes of the *other side* as they prepared for this interaction? If you represented Ace Sporting Goods, what did you think would be the critical factors for the Human Rights Committee? If you represented the Human Rights Committee, why did you think Ace Sporting Goods was willing to negotiate with your organization — and what did you think that firm hoped to get out of this interaction? It is so beneficial for negotiators to try to understand what their opponents want out of impending interactions, to enable them to look for ways they can satisfy the underlying needs of that side at minimal cost to their own side. They should also look for things they wish to obtain that the other side is probably willing to give them.

Negotiators can use the Efficiency Grid set forth on the following page to determine the degree to which they maximized the joint returns achieved by the parties. Less efficient groups should ask themselves what they might have done differently to generate more efficient agreements. What do they think contributed to their less efficient results? Did one or both sides behave in a Competitive/Adversarial manner which minimized the exploration of underlying party interests and diminished the likelihood the parties would discover and exploit areas for joint gains?

ACE SPORTING GOODS — HUMAN RIGHTS COMMITTEE
EFFICIENCY POINTS

	ACE SPORTING GOODS	HUMAN RIGHTS COMM.
ELIM. CHILD LABOR	+25	+30
ELIM. SLAVE LABOR	+25	+30
NO PLANTS IN HUMAN RTS. VIOLATOR NATIONS	+50	+75
HEALTHFUL/SAFE CONDS.	+25	+50
AVERAGE WAGES	0	+25
125% WAGES	-50	+50
150% WAGES	-75	+75
175% WAGES	-100	+100
200% WAGES	-150	+125
225% WAGES	-200	+150
OVER 225% WAGES	-500	+200
ACE HR DEPT. MONITORING	+25	0
HUMAN RTS. COMM. MONITORS	-25	+50
$50,000 LIQ. DAM.	-50	+50
$75,000 LIQ. DAM.	-75	+75
$100,000 LIQ. DAM.	-100	+100
$125,000 LIQ. DAM.	-150	+125
$150,000 LIQ. DAM.	-200	+150
OVER $150,000 LIQ. DAM.	-500	+200
ACE/HUM. RTS. PRESS RE-LEASE	+50	+50
JOINT PRESS CONF.	+50	+50

Chapter 17
MULTI-PARTY NEGOTIATIONS

Although the vast majority of legal negotiations involve two parties interacting with each other, there are occasions when more than two parties are involved. Such multi-party interactions can become quite complex. They tend to involve a number of different issues, and the various participants may value the diverse issues quite differently. A group hierarchy may develop, with the more substantial participants having a greater say in negotiation developments than the less substantial participants. To offset their weaker situations, some parties may form coalitions to enable them to present a united front when they deal with the stronger parties. These coalitions may be general in nature, or they may vary depending upon the specific issues being discusses. Certain parties may work together with respect to some issues, and oppose each other with respect to other issues. In some cases, actual negotiation participants may behave as conciliators working to assist the other participants resolve conflicted issues. Such facilitation is especially likely with respect to issues these particular parties do not feel strongly about.

When group negotiations become contentious, it may be necessary to seek the assistance of external mediators who may use their disinterested positions to work with the disputing parties. They can help the parties define the actual issues in dispute, and work with them to generate mutually acceptable resolutions.

NEGOTIATION EXERCISE

To demonstrate the impact of multi-party negotiations, readers can use the following United Nations Security Council Expansion Exercise. Readers should divide themselves into groups of five persons. One is to represent the United States, another England, another France, another Russia, and the last China — the five permanent members of the Security Council. In recent years, there has been significant pressure on the United Nations to expand the number of permanent members to six, seven, or even eight, and to add members from Asia and Africa.

The individuals representing the Permanent Members should behave as if they are actually the representative of their assigned nations. They should ask themselves how the U.S., Russia, England, France, or China would be likely to vote on the particular changes being contemplated.

UNITED NATIONS SECURITY COUNCIL EXPANSION

The five Permanent Members of the U.N. Security Council have decided to consider possible changes in the structure and membership of the Security Council. World changes, including the break up of the Soviet Union, German unification, and the need to include more diverse representation, have convinced the Permanent Members — China, France, the Russian Federation, the United Kingdom, and the United States — that the time has come to add one or more Permanent Members and possibly modify the status of the current Permanent members.

The fact that four of the five present Permanent Members are considered "white" by other nations has forced the Permanent Members to consider the addition of one or more "non-white" Permanent Members. It is also possible that France and the United Kingdom could be combined (possibly with Germany) to form a single Western European Seat, and/or that the Russian Federation would be combined with former Soviet satellites to form an Eastern European Seat.

The members of each group must assume that they are actually representing the interests of their respective Permanent Member States. They must attempt to determine the manner in which their Nations would wish to have the pertinent issues resolved and must seek to achieve a final agreement that would be acceptable to their particular Countries.

Representatives of the Permanent Member Nations must try to resolve several critical issues:

(1)   Whether to create a single Western European Seat that would jointly represent France and the United Kingdom — and Germany if that nation were granted status equal to that of France and the U.K. If you decide not to create a single Western European Seat, you must determine whether to add Germany as a separate Permanent Council Member.

(2)   Whether to create a single Eastern European Seat that would jointly represent the Russian Federation and the former Soviet satellites.

(3)   Whether to add one or more new Permanent Members — the most likely choices are: Japan (because of its significant economic power); South Africa or Nigeria (due to their importance in Africa); and/or India (due to its emerging economic power).

(4)   Whether to modify the current voting rules that require an affirmative vote of at least nine of the fifteen Council Members on substantive issues — without a single negative vote (*i.e.*, "veto") by a Permanent Member.

You must decide the minimum yes votes of the entire Council needed to approve substantive proposals, and determine whether the Council should continue to allow a single negative vote by a Permanent Member to defeat proposals. [If a Permanent Member abstains, this does **not** defeat the proposal — so long as at least nine other nations vote affirmatively.] If you modify the current single-veto rule (e.g., requiring two or three negative votes by Permanent Members to defeat a proposal), you should specify the minimum number of negative Permanent Member votes needed to defeat substantive proposals.

SELF-ASSESSMENT

SELF-ASSESSMENT

When they begin their deliberations, the different representatives are usually optimistic that they will be able to generate appropriate changes in Security Council rules quickly. As the discussions unfold, however, they begin to appreciate the vastly different political considerations influencing the countries involved. Participants should consider the following Discussion Points and think about how these different factors influenced their group interactions.

(1)   How would each permanent member state view these different issues?

    (A)   Creation of a single **Western European Seat?**

        (1)   How would unified nations — often with different political and/or economic interests — **select** and **instruct** their **representatives?**

        (2)   How would these nations **resolve conflicts** regarding the manner in which their seat is to vote?

    (B)   Creation of a single **Eastern European Seat?**

        (1)   Would **Russia** view this as a **loss of international power?**

        (2)   Would **Russia** view this as a **loss of respect** among its former **satellites?**

    (C)   **Addition** of **new Permanent Members**:

        (1)   Should **new Permanent Members** be **added** to the Security Council?

        (2)   **Which countries** should be **included?**

        (3)   What should the **new voting rules** be with respect to the minimum number of **Permanent Member "no" votes** needed to defeat (*i.e.*, veto) a proposal?

        (4)   Should the new Permanent Members be **denied** any **veto right** with their votes counting the same as traditional non-permanent members?

(2)   What would be the best means of inducing these five nations to resolve these issues in an amicable manner?

(3)   Would it help to have a sixth person function as a negotiation facilitator (*i.e.*, mediator) who would assist the parties to resolve their differences?

Chapter 18
NASA DECISION-MAKING EXERCISE

American Arbitration Association,[*]
Department of Education and Training

Instructions: You are a member of one of two space details assigned to the mission ship "Galaxy," which was originally scheduled to rendezvous with the parent ship "Angel" on the lighted surface of the moon. Due to mechanical difficulties, however, the Galaxy was forced to land on the dark side of the moon some 200 miles from the rendezvous point. During piloting and landing, some of the crew and both Detail A and Detail B captains died. Much of the equipment aboard was damaged. No one knows for sure how long the ship's life support systems will last because all gauges were broken. Detail A piloted the mission and Detail B was to explore the surface before returning to the parent ship. *Survival of both Details is crucial.* Below are listed the 15 items left intact and undamaged after landing.

Your *first task* is to *individually rank* the listed items in order of their importance to the survival of the remaining crew of the mission ship, Galaxy. You have ten minutes to perform this function. Place the number 1 by the most important item, the number 2 by the second most important, and so on through number 15, the least important. Even if you cannot internally distinguish between what you consider Number 3 and Number 4 or Number 7 and Number 8, you should try to determine the five most critical items, the five items intermediate in terms of their importance, and the five least important items.

After the fifteen items have been individually ranked, participants will be divided into Details of eight to twelve persons. During this *second stage* of the process, each Detail will meet as a group and try to determine through group consensus how the fifteen items should be ranked in terms of their relative importance. Each Detail should also decide whether — *as a group* — they wish to hike to the Angel to get help or remain behind at the Galaxy to await rescue. The groups will have fifteen minutes to complete this part of the exercise.

In the *third stage* of this exercise — the Inter-Group Negotiation — different Details will be paired and the two groups will have fifteen minutes to decide which entire group will hike to the Angel for assistance and which entire group will remain at the Galaxy. They will also have to decide how to divide the fifteen items between the group that goes and the group that remains.

---

[*] Reprinted by permission of the American Arbitration Association

INVENTORY OF UNDAMAGED MATERIAL

_____	Ten Blankets
_____	100 Cartons of Food Concentrate (20-day Ration for Each Crew Member)
_____	150 Feet of Nylon Rope
_____	Parachute Silk (From Three Parachutes)
_____	One Portable Heating Unit That is Self Lighting
_____	Two .45 Caliber Loaded Pistols
_____	One Case Dehydrated Milk
_____	Three 100 lb. Tanks of Oxygen (Each Tank Holds 20-Day Supply for Each Crew Member
_____	One Stellar Map of the Moon's Constellation
_____	One Life Raft
_____	One Magnetic Compass That Functions on the Moon
_____	Five Gallons of Water (Normally a 10-Day Ration for Each Member of the Crew)
_____	Five Light Flares Containing Their Own Oxidizing Agent
_____	First Aid Kit Containing Injection Needles
_____	Solar-Powered FM Receiver-Transmitter

INTRA-GROUP DECISION BY CONSENSUS

INSTRUCTIONS: This is an exercise in group decision-making. Your Detail is to use the method of group consensus in reaching its decision. This means that the relative ranking for each of the 15 survival items *must* be agreed on by each Detail member before it becomes a part of the group decision. Consensus is difficult to reach. Therefore, not every ranking will meet with everyone's complete approval. Try, as a group, to make each ranking one with which all Detail members can at least partially agree. Your Detail must also decide whether it would prefer to hike to the Angel for help or remain at the Galaxy while the other group goes for assistance. Here are some guides to use in reaching consensus:

1. Avoid arguing for your own individual judgments. Approach the task on the basis of logic.

2. Avoid changing your mind only to reach agreement and avoid conflict. Support only solutions with which you are able to agree somewhat, at least.

3. Avoid "conflict-reducing" techniques such as majority vote, averaging or trading in reaching decisions.

4. View differences of opinion as helpful rather than as hindrances in decision-making.

On the *Modified NASA Consensus Form* set forth on the following page, place the individual rankings made earlier by each group member and indicate how the full Detail has ranked the different items.

MODIFIED NASA EXERCISE — DETAIL CONSENSUS FORM

ITEMS	A	B	C	D	E	F	G	H	AGT
Ten Blankets									
100 Cartons of Food Concentrate									
150 Feet of Nylon Rope									
Parachute Silk of 3 Parachutes									
One Portable Heating Unit									
Two .45 Caliber Loaded Pistols									
One Case of Dehydrated Milk									
Three 100 lb. Tanks of Oxygen									
One Stellar Map of Moon Constel.									
One Life Raft									
One Magnetic Compass									
Five Gallons of Water									
Five Light Flares									
One First Aid Kit									
Solar Powered FM Receiver/Transm.									

INTER-GROUP DECISION BY NEGOTIATION

INSTRUCTIONS:

Detail A will attempt to *survive* while *waiting for help* at the Galaxy.

Detail B will attempt to *survive* and *rendezvous* with the parent ship Angel.

This is an exercise in group decision-making. Both Details are to use the method of group negotiations in reaching its decision. Both Details must decide which one will remain with the disabled mission ship Galaxy (*i.e.*, which group will be designated "Detail A") and which group will endeavor to rendezvous with the parent ship Angel (*i.e.*, which group will be designated "Detail B"). Both groups must also agree upon the division of the inventoried items between Details A and B (*i.e.*, which items will remain with Detail A and which will be taken with Detail B).

Modified NASA Negotiated Agreement Form is provided on the following page to enable you to list the terms of your negotiated agreement.

MODIFIED NASA — NEGOTIATED AGREEMENT FORM

ITEMS	DETAIL A	DETAIL B
Ten Blankets		
100 Cartons of Food Concentrate		
150 Feet of Nylon Rope		
Parachute Silk From Three Parachutes		
One Portable Heating Unit		
Two .45 Caliber Loaded Pistols		
One Case of Dehydrated Milk		
Three 100 lb. Tanks of Oxygen		
One Stellar Map of Moon's Constellation		
One Life Raft		
One Magnetic Compass		
Five Gallons of Water		
Five Light Flares		
One First Aid Kit		
Solar Powered FM Receiver/Transmitter		

SELF-ASSESSMENT

SELF-ASSESSMENT

Although this should be an entirely cooperative exercise in which everyone should work harmoniously together to ensure the survival of everyone, it does not usually work that way. Competitive urges cause some participants to vie for their own positions without considering the possibility that their positions may not be the best for everyone involved. When the two groups have to negotiate with respect to which group goes for assistance and which group remains with the disabled vehicle, most persons indicate a desire to be in the group to hike to the parent vehicle. This creates an immediate conflict. Even if the two groups decide which one will go for help and which one will remain behind, they often fight about the appropriate division of the different items.

The first question concerns how the ***intra-group*** negotiations were conducted. How did the participants within each group act to minimize conflict? Did a facilitative leader emerge who worked to encourage a consensus with respect to the rankings of the different items? How did this person emerge? Was it because of their prior experience, their physical position within the group, their open willingness to serve in this capacity, their unique personal qualifications, or some other factor? Did a "false leader" try to assume control and was rejected by the group?

Once the ***inter-group*** negotiations begin, it is interesting to see whether all of the group members try to participate in the negotiations or whether they select one or two representatives to conduct the interaction. Since most group members generally prefer to go for help, the two groups tend to fight about this issue. On some occasions, one group is authorized to propose a division of the different items between the group that remains and the group that goes, with the other group then having the right to decide whether it wants to remain or go. Other times the two groups work together to divide the items, and they then use rock/paper/scissors to determine which group remains and which goes.

This exercise graphically demonstrates to participants how competitive tendencies can influence seemingly cooperative interactions. This may be important when business partners with seemingly joint interests have to negotiate, and one or both begin to fight for their own interests even when that result may not be optimal for both parties in the long run. This factor can influence negotiations conducted on behalf of large corporations, government agencies, or private associations. Representatives may initially assume monolithic entities, but quickly appreciate how different departments and divisions fight for their *own interests* regardless of whether this approach is best for the overall organization.

Chapter 19
MEDIATION

The vast majority of law suits are resolved through negotiated settlements, with fewer than two percent of federal civil matters being adjudicated and only 5 to 10 percent of state civil suits being resolved by trial. Most business deals are similarly achieved through inter-party negotiations, as are most inter-government and private-government interactions. When direct party-to-party negotiations do not generate mutual accords, many parties give up and accept their nonsettlement alternatives. They engage in financially and emotionally costly litigation, or forego what might have been mutually beneficial business deals. When such parties are unable to achieve agreements on their own, they should consider mediation assistance that might allow neutral facilitators to help them reach desired results.[1]

Effective mediation can have several highly beneficial effects. Agreements achieved can avoid the monetary and psychological costs associated with trials. Even when disputes are not resolved until the eve of trials, both trial and post-trial proceedings are avoided. Litigation tends to be ***backward looking***, as the parties fight to determine which one was "right," while mediation is ***forward looking*** as the parties work to resolve their differences and move forward with their lives. Mediation can be a ***cathartic process*** which enables the parties to express their emotional feelings to each other in controlled environments. Meditation also allows the parties to control their own destinies, instead of having resolutions imposed upon them by judges, juries, or arbitrators. People usually feel more satisfied with terms they have had the opportunity to structure than with terms imposed upon them by others.

The inability of negotiating parties to achieve mutual accords does not mean that they are better off without agreements. Inexperienced participants may have failed to initiate the negotiation process, fearing that if they raised the possibility of discussions first it would indicate weakness on their part. One or both sides may have employed negotiation tactics that discouraged their opponents. One or both may have over- or under-stated their actual goals to such an extent neither could back down without appearing weak. Communication channels may have been adversely affected because of intense pressure on the participants, or cultural differences may have caused misunderstandings. If these bargaining difficulties could be alleviated, the parties might still be able to reach mutually acceptable terms.

Parties who are unable to achieve their own agreements may often benefit from the assistance of proficient mediators who can help them to regenerate stalled negotiations. Some attorneys may be hesitant to employ mediation, fearing that such sessions may be time-consuming, costly, or result in the imposition of disadvantageous terms. Such trepidations are usually incorrect. The effective use of mediation can actually be cost effective. Litigants can avoid the substantial monetary and psychological costs of trial, while transactional negotiators can prevent the loss of mutually beneficial deals.

Negotiators need not fear that mediators will impose disadvantageous terms upon them or their clients. Mediators lack such authority. They are only empowered to *assist* the parties with *their own* negotiations. They may enhance communication

---

[1] *See generally* LAURENCE J. BOULLE, MICHAEL T. COLATRELLA JR. & ANTHONY P. PICCHIONI, MEDIATION SKILLS AND TECHNIQUES (2008); DWIGHT GOLANN, MEDIATING LEGAL DISPUTES (2009); CHRISTOPHER W. MOORE, THE MEDIATION PROCESS (2003); AMERICAN ARBITRATION ASSN., HANDBOOK ON MEDIATION (2d ed. 2010); JAY FOLBERG & ALISON TAYLOR, MEDIATION (1984).

exchanges and generate innovative options the parties may have not yet contemplated, but the **final authority** over any agreements always rests with the **parties themselves**. Mediators who violate this basic principle and seek to impose terms on unreceptive parties are likely to generate quick impasses.

People often ask mediators what they do when they mediate, and most reply that they employ their *negotiation skills* to assist the parties with their own discussions. What provides mediators with power concerns their detached status and the fact they cannot tell the parties what they must do. They can ask questions and raise issues the parties might feel hesitant to address if they were raised by their opponents.

During the mediation process, the six basic negotiation stages remain the same. The parties — and the mediator — must prepare for their interaction. There is usually a brief Preliminary Stage during which the parties and the mediator become acquainted and the mediator explains the role mediators play. Most neutrals explain the confidentiality of mediation sessions and their neutral function. Most emphasize the fact they have absolutely no authority to tell the parties what to do. Dispute mediators often talk about the fact that litigation is **backward looking**, with the parties using the court or arbitrator to determine which one was right. Mediation, on the other hand, tends to be **forward looking**, with the participants endeavoring to resolve their dispute and get on with their lives.

The participants then engage in an Information Exchange to apprise the neutral facilitator of the issues involved. They then move into the Distributive Stage as they seek to achieve a possible settlement. If this part of the interaction progresses well, the parties see an agreement on the horizon and enter the Closing Stage where they try to reach a mutual accord. If the negotiation includes multiple issues, they should finally move into the Cooperative Stage to see if they can expand the overall pie to be divided between them and simultaneously enhance their respective positions.

When negotiating parties approach or reach impasse, they are usually focusing on their areas of disagreement. They become locked into stated positions, with neither willing to budge for fear of appearing malleable. Neutral facilitators seek to move the parties away from their stated positions and to induce them to explore their underlying interests and alternative solutions.

I. MEDIATOR STYLES

Skilled mediators possess many common qualities no matter which style they employ. They are usually objective and fair-minded individuals. They possess good communication skills — they are good, empathetic listeners and assertive speakers. Most are adept readers of nonverbal signals. They possess good interpersonal skills that enable them to interact effectively with persons with diverse personalities. They also understand the negotiation process, and the ways in which they can enhance that process.

Both neutrals and advocates must appreciate the fact that mediator personalities influence mediator behavior. Assertive and aggressive individuals tend to be more direct mediators, while less assertive and more passive persons tend to be more laid back. People endeavoring to learn mediation skills should try to select a style that is consistent with their own personalities. They should not simply try to emulate the work of others who may have very different demeanors.

Most mediators employ one of three different styles. Facilitative/Elicitive mediators try to reopen blocked communication channels and generate direct inter-party discussions that will enable the parties to formulate their own agreements.

Directive/Evaluative mediators tend to focus more on the substantive terms involved. They try to determine what terms would be acceptable to the parties and convince the parties to accept those terms. An innovative group of mediators are Transformative. They work to demonstrate to participants that they possess power over their final outcomes and to generate mutual respect between the parties that will enhance their ability to solve their own problems.

A.   Facilitative/Elicitive Mediators

These conciliators tend to be process-oriented. They hope to regenerate party-to-party discussions that will enable the parties to structure their own agreements. They view impasses as the result of communication breakdowns and/or unrealistic party expectations. They work to reopen communication channels and to induce advocates to reconsider the reasonable ness of their respective positions. They are elicitive in the way they use questions to generate positional reassessments and to get parties to consider innovative options. They prefer joint sessions during which they try to induce the parties to engage in more open face-to-face discussions. They resort to separate caucus sessions only when they conclude that face-to-face talks are not progressing well.

These mediators ask many questions that are designed to induce the parties to evaluate the reasonableness of their stated positions and to explore underlying party interests. They try to get participants to look behind their stated positions in an effort to appreciate the availability of alternatives that may prove to be mutually beneficial. Whenever possible, they get the parties talking and remain quiet while the parties interact.

B.   Directive/Evaluative Mediators

These neutrals are used to interacting with inexperienced negotiators who have difficulty reaching their own agreements. They often encounter advocates who do not know how to initiate meaningful negotiations or who are unable to explore the different issues in a manner likely to generate mutual accords. These individuals tend to feel a need to control the bargaining interactions they encounter. Judicial mediators frequently employ this style, because they are used to telling litigants what to do and they lack the patience to allow the mediation process to continue for prolonged periods.

Transactions conducted by Directive/Evaluative mediators tend to resemble "parent"-"child" interactions. The "parent"-like neutrals attempt to ascertain the real needs and interests of the "child"-like advocates so they can let those persons know what they *should* accept. These mediators often resort to separate caucus sessions that will enable them to find out confidentially what the participants need to achieve. They then look for formulations that should be mutually acceptable and work to convince the parties that these are the terms they should accept.

Directive/Evaluative mediators do not hesitate to let the parties know how they feel about specific positions being taken. They will suggest which terms are reasonable and which are unreasonable. These substantive-oriented neutrals act as "deal makers" who try to determine what terms would be best for the parties. Although some people think these mediators try to impose their own terms on the parties, this is not really accurate. They try to discover the terms the parties would be likely to accept, then work to convince the participants that these are the terms that would be best for them.

C. Transformative Mediators

Robert Baruch Bush and Joseph P. Folger, in *The Promise of Mediation* (1994)[2], explored an innovative conciliation style which was primarily relationship-oriented. Unlike most traditional mediators whose primary objective concerns final agreements, transformative mediators do not worry about the resolution of the immediate disputes. They believe that mediators should work to *empower* weaker parties my demonstrating to them that they have nonsettlement options they can accept if this alternative becomes necessary. By using this approach to empower parties, they hope to induce those individuals to explore the underlying issues and look for mutually beneficial agreements. They also wish to teach negotiators how to use their abilities to resolve future controversies.

Transformative mediators also work to generate mutual respect between the parties. They do this through *"recognition"* which involves efforts designed to induce each party to respect the interests of the other party. They work to generate inter-party empathy resulting from their efforts to get both sides to appreciate the feelings and perspectives of each other. Instead of focusing primarily on the bargaining process, as do Facilitative/Elicitive mediators, or on substantive issues, as do Directive/Evaluative mediators, Transformative neutrals focus on the disputants themselves. They work to demonstrate to emotionally drained parties that they have options they can effectively pursue if the current discussions do not prove fruitful.

Some traditional mediators claim that they can be both facilitative and transformative mediators by focusing on both the present negotiations *and* the relationship between the parties. Bush and Folger maintain that this approach is not really possible, on the ground that mediators must be interested primarily in either the substantive discussions and the parties' efforts to achieve mutually acceptable terms *or* the ability of the parties to become empowered and resolve their own disputes.

II. INITIATION OF MEDIATION PROCESS

The mediation process may be initiated by court rules, one or more of the parties involved, by referrals from secondary parties, or by appointment by an external agency. If the bargaining participants have any say in mediator selection, they should decide what style of mediation they prefer. Skilled negotiators who merely wish to obtain bargaining assistance should opt for a facilitative/elicitive neutral. Less proficient negotiators who need assistance with their bargaining interaction may prefer a evalutive/directive person. Individuals who will have to deal with each other in the future — such as business partners or spouses getting divorced who have to deal with each other over children — may prefer a transformative individual who will work to preserve their relationship even if the immediate controversy is not resolved through negotiations.

The timing of mediation initiation can be critical. If mediation begins too soon, the parties may not be ready for meaningful discussions and the bargaining process may break down. On the other hand, if mediation begins so late that the parties have locked themselves into unyielding positions they are unlikely to modify, neutral intervention may be ineffective. The optimal time to commence mediation is after the parties have become thoroughly familiar with the underlying issues and have engaged

---

[2] *See also* ROBERT BARUCH BUSH & JOSEPH P. FOLGER, THE PROMISE OF MEDIATION (2d. ed. 2005) (exploring the responses to their 1994 book).

in serious discussions, but before they have reached a complete impasse. This permits the neutral facilitator to become involved while there is still a real opportunity to induce the parties to reconsider their current positions.

III. PREPARATION FOR MEDIATION SESSIONS

Both negotiating parties and designated neutrals should prepare for their interactions. Even if the parties have prepared for their own negotiations, they need to reassess their respective situations in light of the intervention of a neutral facilitator. They should review their current positions to see if they can continue to support those positions rationally. They must next decide how they plan to interact with the mediator. Based upon that person's style, what approach do they think will be most effective? How much are they willing to disclose at joint sessions with the other side, and what are they willing to disclose in confidential separate caucus sessions with the mediator? They should try to go behind the stated positions of their side and of the other side to look for alternatives that might proved to be mutually beneficial. They should try to approach the mediated sessions with as open a mind as possible.

Many mediation rules require the actual clients to be present at the initial — and sometimes subsequent — mediation sessions. It thus becomes imperative for lawyers to prepare their clients for such sessions. The clients should be prepared for mediator comments they might find intimidating — especially where judicial officers are serving as the negotiation facilitators — since such persons tend to be rather directive/evaluative. They are used to telling parties what to do, and that predisposition carries over to their mediation encounters. The clients should know when it is beneficial for them to speak and when they should allow their advocates to speak for them. If the mediators ask to meet with the clients alone, the attorneys should carefully prepare the clients for such encounters.

The selected mediator should also try to prepare for the upcoming sessions. She should ask the parties to provide her with copies of relevant documents that would assist her to appreciate their current positions. When she first contacts the parties individually — often by telephone — she should not hesitate to ask each what the dispute is about and their current positions. She needs to begin to appreciate the underlying interests and the possible alternatives that might be beneficially explored during face-to-face party discussions. The more the mediator knows prior to the initial formal session, the easier it tends for her to begin the discussions beneficially.

IV. CONDUCTING MEDIATION SESSIONS

Mediators generally conduct their sessions at neutral locations — the mediator's own office or another non-party site. They prefer meeting arrangements that have sufficient room for all of the participants, with separate rooms for caucus sessions if they become necessary. Many mediators try to arrange the furniture in a non-confrontational configuration. Some use round tables to avoid having the parties sit directly across from each other in a confrontational setting. Even where square or rectangular tables are involved, mediators can deal with this issue by sitting on one side of the table and asking the parties to sit next to each other along the other side. This is a more cooperative configuration, and it encourages the parties to think mentally that they are on the same side.

Most mediators conduct an initial joint session with the attorneys and the clients present to be certain that all of the relevant parties understand the mediation process and the issues underlying the current matter. After the parties are all introduced, the mediators explain their neutral facilitation function. Most emphasize the fact they have no power to tell the parties what to do; they are only there to assist the parties achieve their own agreement. Mediators stress the confidentiality of the mediation process. They also indicate that if separate caucus sessions are conducted, the information shared with them by the parties during such sessions will not be disclosed to the other side without their consent.

After the preliminary explanation of the mediation process, mediators usually ask the parties to summarize the issues to be addressed. Opposing parties are asked not to interrupt, to provide each side with the opportunity to set forth their positions without direct conflict. Facilitative/Elicitive mediators tend to use questions to generate party discussions. They ask each party questions designed to induce them to appreciate their weaknesses and to rethink the appropriateness of their stated positions. Directive/Evaluative mediators tend to be more direct. They are more likely to indicate their own view of party positions. Transformative mediators ask parties questions designed to demonstrate that they possess viable nonsettlement options they can rely upon if the present discussions to not culminate in mutual accords. They also work to induce each side to have an appreciation for the other side's perspective, even if they do not agree with it to develop a degree of mutual respect.

Where legal disputes are involved, mediators try to ask both parties questions designed to emphasize party weaknesses. Claimants may be asked if there is a possibility they may not prevail at trial, to induce them to think of their *down-side risk*. Defendants, on the other hand, may be asked about the possibility the claimant might prevail and the possible outcomes if the claimant does to induce them to contemplate their *up-side risk*. The parties are also asked about potential transaction costs, recognizing that claimants must *subtract* those costs from anything they obtain, while defendants must *add* those costs to anything they must pay.This factor helps to move the parties toward one another.

When transactional interactions are involved, the mediators work to bring the parties closer together. Most ask questions designed to lower the demands being made by one side and to increase the offers being made by the other. Questions are used to explore the underlying needs and interests of the parties to look for ways the parties can expand the overall pie to be divided to maximize the joint returns achieved. By the time mediation is requested by transactional negotiators, the parties tend to be focused almost entirely on their areas of dispute. Skilled mediators try to change the focus from those distributive items to more cooperative items that the parties can exchange and simultaneously improve their respective positions. This technique gets the parties saying "yes" to each other. As they tentatively agree upon these different issues, they become psychologically committed to overall agreements. When they finally return to the more controverted items, they no longer seem as insurmountable as they did when the parties were at impasse. In addition, the parties have found many areas for joint gains, and they do not wish to have those tentative agreements lost at this point in the process.

Where emotional issues are involved, skilled neutrals can use joint sessions to allow cathartic venting in controlled environments. The upset parties are permitted to express their underlying feelings candidly, but without intemperate personal attacks that would only exacerbate the situation. After such disclosures, the other side may be encouraged to apologize in a manner designed to offset the emotional feelings that have been expressed. They may merely indicate how sorry this situation has arisen or how sorry they are the other side feels the way they do. Such expressions can significantly diminish the negative emotions felt by the other side.

Disputing parties frequently characterize critical issues in one-sided terms designed to support their own interests. Neutral facilitators can often get them to reframe these issues in more neutral terms that will enable the parties to explore their different issues in a more detached fashion. Role reversals are occasionally employed to induce the parties to appreciate the positions being taken by each other. For example, a prospective business seller might be asked to evaluate the firm from a prospective purchaser's perspective, and the prospective buyer could be asked to assess the circumstances from the firm owner's perspective.

When joint sessions seem to be moving toward irreconcilable positions, it can be beneficial for mediators to ask the parties if they would be willing to allow separate caucus sessions designed to let the mediators to explore the underlying issues more candidly with each party. As each separate session begins, the mediators should reiterate the confidential nature of these sessions. They should then ask each party what they should know that they do not already know. This question is designed to get the parties talking about matters they have been unwilling to discuss in the presence of the other side. Some party concerns may not be that significant, and the neutrals can try to get the parties to appreciate this fact. Other concerns may be quite real, and the mediators have to explore them carefully with the parties in ways that may enable them to look for ways to resolve them appropriately. Each side is asked where they might be willing to modify their current positions, as the mediators look for ways to narrow the gaps between the different party positions.

Mediators should constantly look for issues the parties value differently. This permits item exchanges that enhance the underlying needs of both sides. Where distributive issues are involved, mediators may use **conditional offers** where each party is asked if it would agree to move closer to the other side if that side simultaneously moved toward it. Even where the quintessential distributive item — money — is involved, it can be converted into a less controversial matter by asking the parties to contemplate structured deals calling for payments made over many years or in-kind payments where goods or services are provided in lieu of cash.

During both litigation mediation and transactional mediation, it is important for neutral facilitators to make it appear that the parties are moving together. This appearance of fairness can be crucial if the parties hope to achieve acceptable agreements. It is also important for the parties to feel they were treated respectfully by both the mediator and the other side during conciliation sessions. Such an approach is likely to generate greater party satisfaction at the conclusion of the process, no matter how objectively beneficial the actual terms may be.

MEDIATION EXERCISE

Readers should form groups of three. One should be designated Side A, one Side B, and one the Mediator. They can work on one of the exercises in this book or on one set forth in the Teacher's Manual. All three persons should receive the General Information. The Side A representatives also get that side's Confidential Information, and the Side B representatives get that side's Confidential Information. The Mediators get neither side's Confidential Information.

The groups of three should be given 40–45 minutes to reach an agreement settling their dispute. During the first ten minutes of the interactions, only the Side A and Side B representatives may speak. The Mediators are present and may listen to what is being said, but they may not speak during this initial ten minute period. After that time period, the mediators may become active participants in the discussions. They should use the techniques they think that mediators would employ to help the parties generate final accords.

SELF-ASSESSMENT

SELF-ASSESSMENT

After the final agreements have been achieved — or impasses have occurred — the participants should conduct postmortems. They should consider the degree to which they though the mediator assistance facilitated their interactions. What did the neutral persons do to minimize party conflict and induce the parties to explore the underlying issues in a mutually beneficial manner? What did the mediators do that they did not find helpful? What else do they think the Mediators could have done to encourage settlements more effectively? Mediators should be asked why they employed certain approaches and what other approaches they might have used more effectively.

Chapter 20
ETHICAL DILEMMAS

When I teach negotiation courses to law students and attorneys, I often begin by indicating that I have never participated in professional negotiations during which both sides did not lie, yet I have encountered very few negotiators I thought were dishonest. How can negotiators lie without being dishonest? They misrepresent matters they are not expected to discuss truthfully.

Two people get together to negotiate. One is authorized to accept any amount over $100,000, while the other is authorized to pay up to $130,000. They thus have a $30,000 settlement range between their respective bottom lines. They initially exchange small talk, then begin to explore the substantive issues of their exchange. The person who hopes to obtain money states that he cannot accept anything below $150,000, while the person willing to pay money indicates that she cannot go a penny over $70,000. They are pleased to have begun their interaction successfully, yet both have begun with bold-faced lies! Have they committed ethical violations?

Model Rule 4.1 provides that an attorney "shall not knowingly: (a) make a false statement of material fact or law to a third person." This unequivocally indicates that lawyers may not lie. When is a lie not a lie, when it's by a lawyer! When this rule was being drafted, people who teach negotiation skills pointed out that if all misrepresentations were forbidden, most negotiating attorneys would be subject to discipline because of what is euphemistically characterized as "puffing" or "embellishment." As a result, Reporter's Comment 2 was included with Rule 4.1 indicating that different expectations are involved when attorneys negotiate.

> Whether a particular statement should be regarded as one of fact can depend on the circumstances. Under generally accepted conventions in negotiation, certain types of statements ordinarily are not taken as statements of material fact. Estimates of price or value placed on the subject of a transaction and a party's intentions as to an acceptable settlement of a claim are in this category.

As a result, if one party offered to pay the other $115,000, the offer recipient could ethically indicate that this sum was unacceptable to his side even though he knew it was perfectly acceptable.[1]

Comment 2 not only permits attorneys to misrepresent their side's **settlement intentions**, but also the way in which they subjectively **value the items** being exchanged. For example, if the other side requested a non-admission provision indicating that her side wished to disclaim any admission of legal responsibility for what was being resolved, the first party could oppose such a provision even though he knows that his client does not care about such a provision. He may do this in an effort to obtain more money for his client in exchange for the non-admission clause the other side values. Both of these statements are considered "puffing" since they pertain to nonmaterial information.

Most lawyers have no difficulty with the Reporter's Comment indicating that statements concerning one's actual settlement intentions and the subjective value placed on items being exchanged do not have to be truthful. They pertain to "puffing"

---

[1] Under Rule 1.4, he would have an ethical duty to convey such an offer to his client, unless it was already clear that the amount in question was unacceptable to the client. Under Rule 1.2, the attorney would also be obliged to abide by his client's decision whether to accept or reject the offer in question.

and "embellishment," and do not involve matters one expects to be discussed with complete candor.[2] On the other hand, it is strange to suggest that these matters do not concern "material fact." When lawyers negotiate, the factual, legal, economic, and political issues underlying the instant transaction are really secondary. What parties have to determine through the negotiation process is how the other side values the items being exchanged and how much of each must be offered to induce the other side to enter into an agreement. Nonetheless, attorneys generally expect such "puffing" during bargaining encounters and are not offended by persons who over- or under-state the value of items for strategic purposes or who are not entirely forthright regarding their true settlement intentions.

The principal difficulty professional organizations have regulating the behavior of negotiators concerns the unique circumstances in which most bargaining interactions are conducted. They are usually done on a one-on-one basis in person or over the telephone. If one person is a lying scoundrel and they are accused of dishonesty by another party, they lie to the disciplinary authority. It is extremely difficult for such a body to determine which side is telling the truth. What really regulates this area is the market place. If persons behave in a questionable manner, their reputations will be quickly tarnished. When someone encounters others who lie about what they have the right to know, they usually tell their friends and associates. They may even post something regarding that person's lack of ethics on the Internet. Those deceivers begin to encounter difficulties when they negotiate. Individuals do not trust them. Their statements have to be independently verified, and their agreements have to be reduced to writing. Their negotiations become more cumbersome and less efficient. If they try to regain reputations for honesty, they discover how difficult it is to overcome stories about their past. Any negotiator who contemplates improper behavior during bargaining interactions should appreciate the substantial risks involved. A short-term gain may easily become a long-term stumbling block to future deals.

The three basic areas of misrepresentations concern affirmative misrepresentations, truthful statements that are incomplete and misleading, and the failure to disclose information necessary to prevent misunderstandings by the other side.

I. AFFIRMATIVE FACTUAL MISREPRESENTATIONS

Suppose a client is thinking of selling her company and another party has approached her attorney to discuss their possible purchase of this firm. Assume that the corporate owner has told her negotiator that she would like to get at least $50 million, but might go as low as $45 million, if necessary. The prospective buyer asks how much it would take to buy this firm. Can her lawyer ethically suggest $60 million? Clearly the answer is yes, because this statement pertains to non-material information — their settlement intentions — and is considered acceptable "puffing." The prospective buyer then offers $35 million, and the seller's representative asks if they would consider going higher. Could the prospective buyer's attorney ethically suggest an unwillingness to increase his offer even if he knows his client would be willing to do so? Again yes, since this is still "puffing."

Could the seller's attorney suggest that others would probably be interested in her client's firm? Unless it was unequivocally clear that no one else could possibly be interested, such a statement would undoubtedly be considered acceptable "puffing."

---

[2] *See* Charles B. Craver, *Negotiation Ethics for Real World Interactions*, 25 Ohio St. J. Disp. Res. 299 (2010).

If no one else has indicated an interest in the seller's business, could the seller's representative ethically indicate that other parties have made actual offers? Although I have had a few attorneys suggest that this type of statement is mere "puffing," I do not agree. I think this is highly material fact information that must be discussed honestly if it is mentioned at all. As a result, if the seller's attorney states that other prospective buyers have tendered offers, that person has to convey truthful information. If another party has offered $40 million, could the seller's attorney ethically state that she has been offered $50 million? Since I consider this to be material fact information this possible buyer has the right to rely upon, I do not believe she can make such a misrepresentation. She might, however, avoid the ethical dilemma by indicating that they have received another offer, and by stating that someone will have to pay $50 million of they wish to purchase the company. She is not disclosing what offer has actually been received, but is only indicating — truthfully — that another offer has been tendered. Without disclosing the actual amount involved, she is merely stating that it will take $50 million to buy the company. Even if her client is willing to sell for less, this is nonmaterial "puffing."

To what degree may attorneys overstate the true value of the company their client is selling? May they suggest it has a rosy future, even if that is not entirely clear? May they say the firm is on the verge of an important product development when that is incorrect? May they indicate that the firm has accounts receivable of $540,000, when those accounts total only $150,000? The first statement of a wholly subjective nature is probably acceptable if they do not embellish too greatly. The other two representations would be improper, because they concern material fact information the other party has the right to rely upon. While they may have no affirmative obligation to disclose these facts, if they choose to discuss them, they must do so honestly.

II. PARTIALLY TRUTHFUL FACTUAL STATEMENTS

Some seemingly truthful statements can be misleading. Suppose someone is thinking of purchasing a house that suffered substantial damage in a hurricane, but seems to have been restored. What if the prospective purchaser asks if the storm damage has been repaired? Could the seller truthfully indicate that the roof has been completely replaced, but say nothing about the fact the eves under the roof still leak when it rains? Since it should be apparent that the person hearing this representation would be likely to assume that the storm damage has been entirely repaired, the seller should either have to remain silent or include information indicating that additional leaks exist. In many states requiring house sellers to disclose known defects of a serious nature, the seller would be obliged to disclose the leaking eves even if they are not specifically asked about this issue. Comment 1 to Rule 4.1 expressly recognizes that a "misrepresentation can also occur by partially true but misleading statements or omissions that are the equivalent of affirmative false statements." Ethical opinions have thus held that truthful statements may constitute actionable misrepresentations when they are made under circumstances in which the person making the statements knows the other party is misinterpreting what is being conveyed.

When negotiators are asked about delicate issues or decide to raise those matters on their own, their statements should be phrased in a manner that conveys — both explicitly and implicitly — truthful information. They should not use half-truths they know are likely to induce listeners to misunderstand the actual circumstances. If they are not sure what to say, they may remain silent. If they choose to speak, however, they must do so in a way that is not misleading.

III. IMPERMISSIBLE FACTUAL OMISSIONS

In many business and legal interactions the basic rule is *caveat emptor* — buyer beware. If the buyer does not ask the right questions and the seller makes no affirmative misrepresentations, the buyer has no recourse if he subsequently discovers problems. When might seller silence give rise to legal liability? Whenever the law imposes an affirmative duty to disclose. As noted above, the laws in many states require home sellers to disclose known defects of a serious nature. Sellers who fail to satisfy this duty may be sued for the damages caused by the undisclosed defects.

Similar affirmative duties are imposed upon stock and bond sellers by securities laws. Before selling stocks or bonds to buyers, owners are required to provide prospectuses that include detailed financial information. If they fail to include relevant positive and negative information, they can be held liable for their omissions.

IV. LEGAL MISREPRESENTATIONS AND OMISSIONS

When negotiators interact in the legal arena, they almost always discuss relevant statutes, regulations, and judicial decisions. Side A emphasizes the doctrines supportive of its position, while Side B cites the rules supporting its position. It is clear that neither side may knowingly make a false statement of material law without violating the proscription set forth in Rule 4.1.[3] On the other hand, Rule 4.1 does not require attorneys to provide opposing counsel with citations supportive of that side's situation. If Side B representatives fail to discover applicable code provisions or case law supporting their circumstances, almost no lawyers feel obliged to provide them with the missing citations. They maintain that it is the duty of the other side's lawyers to locate these references, and if they fail to do so these attorneys feel no need to assist them. They must merely refrain from any representations that would be contrary to the legal doctrines they know exist. On the other hand, if they are litigators and the matter in dispute ends up in court, Rule 3.3(a)(2) provides that "A lawyer shall not knowingly: (2) fail to disclose to the tribunal legal authority in the controlling jurisdiction known to the lawyer to be directly adverse to the position of the client and not disclosed by opposing counsel." They must thus apprise the court of the citations supporting the position of their adversary.

V. UNCONSCIONABLE NEGOTIATING TACTICS

In recent years, a number of lawyers — especially in larger urban areas — have decided to employ highly offensive tactics to advance client interests. They are often rude or nasty. These persons erroneously equate discourteous actions with effective advocacy. Such inappropriate tactics are actually a substitute for proficient lawyering skill. Competent practitioners realize that impolite behavior is the antithesis of effective representation. Although Model Rule 1.3 provides that "[a] lawyer shall act with reasonable diligence and promptness in representing a client," Comment 1 specifically states that "[t]he lawyer's duty to act with reasonable diligence does not

---

[3] Litigators are under a similar obligation under Rule 3.3(a)(1) to refrain from making any false statement of law (or fact) to a tribunal — whether material or not.

require the use of offensive tactics or preclude the treating of all persons involved in the legal process with courtesy and respect."

Legal representatives should eschew tactics that are merely designed to humiliate or harass opponents. Model Rule 4.4 expressly states that "a lawyer shall not use means that have no substantial purpose other than to embarrass, delay, or burden a third person . . ." Demented win-lose negotiators may endeavor to achieve total annihilation of adversaries through the degradation of opposing counsel. Not only is such behavior morally reprehensible, but it needlessly exposes the offensive perpetrators to future recriminations that could easily be avoided through common courtesy. In litigation situations, it might also expose the offensive actors to judicial sanctions. This approach guarantees the offensive actors far more nonsettlements than would be experienced by their more cooperative cohorts.

VI. INTERACTIONS WITH NEUTRAL FACILITATORS

When lawyers representing clients interact with judicial settlement facilitators or private mediators, may they puff and embellish as they can with opposing attorneys pursuant to Comment 2 to Rule 4.1? *ABA Formal Opin.* 93-370 (1993) indicated that knowing misrepresentations to judicial mediators regarding client settlement intentions and subjective values would be impermissible, based upon the view that the Comment 2 exception only applies to bargaining interactions with *opposing counsel.* Since such misstatements to judicial officials would not be confined to adversarial communications, they would contravene Rule 4.1.

In *ABA Formal Opin.* 06-439 (2006), the ABA had to decide whether the logic of *Formal Opin.* 93-370 (1993) barred puffing and embellishment to nonjudicial mediators. If it followed the reasoning of the 1993 Opinion, lawyers could not misrepresent client settlement intentions and values to all neutral parties, but the ABA felt uncomfortable with such an expansive prohibition. As a result, it decided to limit the coverage of the prior Opinion to judicial officers, and it held that such conversations with judicial settlement facilitators are governed by Model Rule 3.3(a)(1) which forbids lawyers from knowingly making false statements of fact to tribunals. As a result, it held that Comment 2 to Rule 4.1 would still apply to communications between advocates and nonjudicial mediators in separate caucus sessions, allowing the use of traditional puffing and embellishment. I was not surprised by Opinion 06-439, since advocates regularly exaggerate their positions and hide their true values when I initiate settlement discussions as a nonjudicial mediator. Despite the logic of the previous 1993 Opinion, I had always assumed that the Comment 2 exception to Rule 4.1 was applicable to their interactions with me.

VII. CONCLUSION

Although some misrepresentations are considered acceptable "puffing," others are clearly inappropriate. It is not always easy to draw the line between statements the other side does not have the right to rely upon and those they may consider sacrosanct. When my students ask about the proper demarcation, I tell them to ask how they would feel if their opponent were to make the misrepresentation they are contemplating. If they would consider their opponent dishonest, then they should refrain from such conduct themselves. I like to leave them with a quote from Mark Twain: "Always do right. This will gratify some people and astonish the rest."

NEGOTIATION ETHICS EXERCISE

Readers should pair up, with half being designated Plaintiff Parker representatives and half being designated Defendant Davidson representatives They should then work the following negotiation exercise to allow them to struggle with the types of ethical issues lawyers encounter during their bargaining interactions. Everyone should read the General Information, and their own side's Confidential Information. They should think about the degree to which they over- or under-state the seriousness of the claimant's medical problems for strategic purposes. Negotiators should think about their initial and subsequent demands and offers. To what degree have they over- or under-stated those positions? Do they consider their actions mere "puffing" or "embellishment" — or inappropriate deception? Have they explored the operative legal doctrines in a neutral manner, or has each side emphasized the legal concepts supportive of their own positions?

GENERAL INFORMATION — PARKER v. DAVIDSON

Last September 1, at 2:35 p.m., twenty-seven year old Harry Parker was driving south in his three-year old Honda Accord on Wisconsin Avenue in Washington, D.C. This is a four-lane street that carries a substantial amount of traffic between Georgetown and the Maryland suburbs. It was a clear, sunny day, and the pavement was dry. Although the speed limit on that part of Wisconsin Avenue is 25 mph, Mr. Parker was driving 35 mph. As Mr. Parker approached the stop light at R Street, N.W., he observed a green light for southbound traffic and he continued to travel at 35 mph.

John Davidson was driving west on R Street in his new Ford Taurus. He was then employed by the District of Columbia Department of Public Works as a civil engineer. At 1:30 p.m., Mr. Davidson had become embroiled in a disagreement with his immediate supervisor concerning Mr. Davidson's dissatisfaction with the 2 percent salary increase he had recently received. Their discussion had taken more time than he had anticipated. Mr. Davidson was thus late for an important job interview he had scheduled with a private engineering firm. He was hoping to obtain a new position that would pay him almost $10,000 more per year than the $47,500 he was currently earning.

As Mr. Davidson approached Wisconsin Avenue, he was driving 37 mph in a 25 mph zone. When he arrived at the Wisconsin Avenue — R Street intersection, Mr. Davidson noticed that the light for traffic in his direction was red. Mr. Davidson reduced his speed to 25 mph and endeavored to make a right turn onto Wisconsin Avenue. His rate of speed was excessive, and his car swerved into the outer lane of southbound traffic. His car struck the left front portion of Mr. Parker's vehicle, causing that car to veer into a light pole located just below the south-west corner of the intersection. When Mr. Parker's car struck the light pole, it stopped abruptly.

Mr. Davidson was wearing his seat belt, and his air bag opened as soon as the two vehicles collided. As a result, he suffered no serious injuries. Mr. Parker was also wearing a seat belt, but the air bag in his car did not deploy until it struck the light pole. When his automobile first collided with the Davidson car (and before the air bag opened), his upper chest struck the steering wheel. He sustained a crushing blow to the chest that caused a cracked sternum and multiple rib fractures. Mr. Parker was taken to the Georgetown University Hospital where he was thoroughly examined. They discovered the cracked sternum and the fractured ribs. They taped Mr. Parker's upper body and provided him with medication to reduce his discomfort. Although Mr. Parker's upper body was severely contused, there was no evidence of additional injury. The Emergency Room treatment cost Mr. Parker $1425. His subsequent examinations by Dr. Joan Bannon, an orthopedic specialist, cost an additional $475. He was out of work for two weeks. Mr. Parker is a self-employed electrician, and these two weeks of missed work cost him $2200. Mr. Parker continued to experience some pain for an eight-week period, but he was able to perform his usual job duties after the second week. On October 28, Dr. Bannon examined Mr. Parker and declared him recovered. Mr. Parker's Honda Accord was totally wrecked, at a loss of approximately $12,400.

Last month, Mr. Parker filed a civil action against Mr. Davidson alleging that his negligent driving caused their accident. His complaint requested $100,000. Defendant Davidson carries liability insurance providing $100,000 coverage per accident. The District of Columbia is still a contributory negligence jurisdiction.

CONFIDENTIAL INFORMATION — PLAINTIFF PARKER

CONFIDENTIAL INFORMATION — PLAINTIFF PARKER

Mr. Parker sued Mr. Davidson, because he was angry about the fact that Mr. Davidson did not exhibit any sympathy following the accident. Mr. Davidson had even complained to Mr. Parker about the job opportunity he was going to lose. Since Mr. Parker's chest wounds have completely healed and he experiences only limited discomfort on cold, damp days, he does not expect a substantial sum of money. He would like to obtain at least $16,500 to cover his $1900 in medical expenses, the $12,400 value of his destroyed Honda Accord, and the $2200 in lost earnings. He has indicated that he will accept any amount over $16,500 you believe would be appropriate. Since Mr. Parker's injuries have healed, he does not want to have to take time off from work to participate in a trial. He has thus instructed you to settle this case immediately. If you fail to reach a settlement agreement, you will be placed at the **bottom** of your group.

Three months ago, you had Mr. Parker examined thoroughly by Dr. James Woods, an internist, who indicated that Mr. Parker's cracked sternum and fractured ribs had healed completely. His heart and lungs appear to be functioning properly, with no evidence of any impairment. Last week, the Defense Attorney had Mr. Parker examined by Dr. Jules Goldberg, an orthopedic/thoracic specialist. You anticipate that Dr. Goldberg will testify as an expert witness for the defense and will reiterate Dr. Woods' findings.

CONFIDENTIAL INFORMATION — DEFENDANT DAVIDSON

CONFIDENTIAL INFORMATION — DEFENDANT DAVIDSON

You realize that your client was extremely negligent when he attempted to turn right onto Wisconsin Avenue at an excessive rate of speed and without stopping at the red light. Nonetheless, this is not your primary concern. Although Dr. Joan Bannon, who treated Mr. Parker after the accident, and Dr. James Woods, who examined Mr. Parker three months ago at the request of Plaintiff's Attorney, have indicated that Mr. Parker's chest wounds have completely healed, this is incorrect. Last week, you had Mr. Parker examined by Dr. Jules Goldberg, an orthopedic/thoracic specialist. Dr. Goldberg agreed that the cracked sternum and the fractured ribs had healed, but he discovered the early formation of an aorta aneurysm. Dr. Goldberg noted that the X-rays taken of Mr. Parker in the Georgetown University Hospital did not include any evidence of an aneurysm. The X-rays subsequently taken by Dr. Woods, an internal medicine specialist, did not appear to indicate the presence of an aneurysm. Only when Dr. Goldberg reviewed the Woods' X-rays with a magnifying glass in light of his recent findings did he notice the incipient formation of an aorta aneurysm. His recent X-rays indicate that the aneurysm has progressed. If it remains untreated, it could rupture and cause the death of Mr. Parker. Since the aneurysm was not evident in the Georgetown University Hospital X-rays, and has increased in size since then, Dr. Goldberg is convinced that the crushing chest injury inflicted in the September 1 automobile accident with Mr. Davidson caused that condition.

In light of Dr. Goldberg's medical conclusions, Mr. Davidson's insurance carrier would like to settle this suit expeditiously. Neither Mr. Parker nor his attorney is aware of Dr. Goldberg's findings with respect to the aorta aneurysm. If they have additional X-rays taken before trial, they would most likely discover his serious condition. If the aneurysm did not exist, you would probably be able to settle this case for $20,000 to $25,000. If Mr. Parker's attorney was aware of the aneurysm, he would undoubtedly demand a figure ten times that range, since Mr. Parker may need surgery to correct his condition. That delicate medical procedure would be expensive, and the recovery period would be fairly long. Mr. Parker would experience prolonged discomfort, and would likely miss ten to twelve weeks of work.

Your supervisor has instructed you to resolve this matter immediately. He wants to have a complete settlement agreement before Mr. Parker undergoes further medical tests. If you do not resolve this dispute now, you will be placed at the ***bottom*** of your group.

SELF-ASSESSMENT

SELF-ASSESSMENT

Once the participants have completed their negotiation of the *Parker v. Davidson* exercise, the plaintiff representatives should ask themselves if they are aware of the fact their client has a life-threatening condition? Most are not aware of this fact; the few that now possess this information usually obtained it from their opponents *after* the case was settled. Negotiators should initially consider two practical considerations that do not concern ethical issues.

(1) Did the plaintiff representatives **ask** the defendant representatives what Dr. Goldberg had discovered during his examination of Parker? Almost no Plaintiff representatives ever ask this critical question. They should remember that if they ever suspect the other side possesses relevant information, they should **ask about it**. They know their client has been examined by a defense physician. They need to know if that person has discovered anything they do not know. If the other side fails to provide them with a direct response to this question, they should ask it again.

(2) Why would the defense attorneys ask for an independent medical examination when both doctors who have already examined Parker have indicated that everything has healed? Attorneys need to know when *not* to seek more information, when there is a risk they may discover something they do not really wish to know.

Negotiators should then tackle the ethical dilemma faced by defense counsel. Did they have an affirmative duty to voluntarily disclose Parker's aneurism to allow him to obtain immediate treatment? When this exact question arose many years ago in *Spaulding v. Zimmerman*, 263 Minn. 346, 116 N.W.2d 704 (1962), the Minnesota Supreme Court held that under Rule 1.6 governing client confidentiality, the defense attorney not only was under no obligation to disclose the claimant's medical condition — he was actually precluded from disclosing such confidential information, without his client's consent.[4]

If the claimant's attorney asked the defense counsel about the claimant's condition, the defense lawyer could — but was not required to — disclose the aneurism. This right was the quid pro quo for the right of the defense counsel to have an independent medical examination conducted of the plaintiff. If this question were asked, how might the defense attorney deal with it? Could she indicate that everything had healed? Clearly not, since this would be an overt misrepresentation of material fact. Could she say that "the ribs and the sternum have completely healed?" I think the answer is no, because this partially truthful statement clearly implies to the listener that everything is fine. The defense attorney knows this is incorrect and is aware of the fact the plaintiff lawyer is misinterpreting what has been said. Could the defense counsel use a *Blocking Technique* to avoid any direct answer? For example, when asked about Dr. Goldberg's findings, he asks how much lost earnings Parker

---

[4] To circumvent the unfair result the Court thought was caused by this application of Rule 1.6, the Minnesota Supreme Court employed a different device. David Spaulding, the plaintiff in that case, was a minor when it arose. As a result, the settlement he agreed to had to be approved by the trial court. Although nothing was asked or said about Spaulding's aneurism when the settlement was being approved, the Minnesota Supreme Court held that as officers of the court defense counsel had an affirmative duty to disclose the newly discovered medical information to the trial court prior to its approval of the settlement agreement — to avoid the possibility that the court would approve an unconscionable settlement agreement. *See generally* Timothy W. Floyd & John Gallagher, *Legal Ethics, Narrative, and Professional Identity: The Story of David Spaulding*, 59 MERCER L. REV. 941 (2008).

sustained. He might alternatively respond with an offer of $20,000. In both cases, he hopes to divert the claimant attorney's attention from the medical issue to the lost wage issue or to an evaluation of the reasonableness of the $20,000 figure. If this approach is successful, the claimant's attorney may fail to restate this inquiry.

In the mid-1990s, the American Law Institute addressed the *Spaulding v. Zimmerman* issue in Section 66 of the *Restatement (3rd) of the Law Governing Lawyers*. That section provides that lawyers who voluntarily disclose conditions posing a risk of death or serious bodily injury to opponents should not be found in violation of the Rule 1.6 confidentiality provision nor be subject to legal malpractice liability to their own clients. In 2002, the A.B.A. House of Delegates modified Model Rule 1.6 covering client confidentiality to indicate that lawyers *may* — but are still *not required* to — disclose confidential information when such disclosure is necessary to prevent death or serious bodily injury. Although some people thought this modification should have *required* disclosure in such circumstances, mandatory disclosure was rejected. While defense attorneys possessing such negative information cannot ethically misrepresent the operative facts — either directly or through partially truthful statements they know are misleading — they still do not have to volunteer that information. I personally would have preferred a rule that required such disclosure, both because of the moral implications involved and to avoid possible economic harm to attorneys who do the right thing and lose business to lawyers who promise not to disclose such information unless specifically directed to do so by their clients. Although the physician retained by defense counsel as an expert witness would similarly be under no duty to disclose this critical information to Plaintiff Parker, I would suggest that the admonition of the Hippocratic Oath that doctors do no harm should oblige them to make a similar disclosure.